Praise for *Ho*

Lori Desautels shares a new vision for our education system that looks beyond its four walls and politics directly into the hearts, minds, and lives of our children. She takes education in a transformative direction that addresses the urgency of our education system's current challenges, offering intelligent, wise, skillful models whose cost is our willingness to apply them in order to deliver authentic education to our children and our world.

~ Michael Bernard Beckwith, author of
Spiritual Liberation: Fulfilling Your Soul's Potential

Riding the crest of creativity and innovation in education, Dr. Desautels' *How May I Serve You?* is a must-read book that combines theory, pedagogy and personal reflection directed toward helping children grow into inquisitive, resilient, collegial, and emotionally sound adults through advancing happiness, optimism and wellbeing. The author's contention that all education ought to be an education of mind and heart artfully challenges seasoned and novice teachers alike to rise above the current maelstrom of failed school reform and outdated teaching methods to transform children's educational experiences by creating positive changes through mindful intelligence and brain-based learning.

~ Dr. Marc A. Meyer, Director of Education,
The Hawn Foundation

Lori Desautels leads from the heart in her narrative of human potential. *How May I Serve You?* is a poignant imperative calling us into vulnerability: for a better life realized, we must give ourselves over to the well-being of others. Lori's voice is clear and pure.

If we have courage, if we follow from the heart, we will be beckoned.

~ Lindan B. Hill, Ph.D
Dean, School of Education, Marian University
Director, Marian University Academy for
Teaching and Learning Leadership

What if students and educators could begin to feel understood and capable when walking through the doors of public, charter and private schools, entering their world of classrooms with enthusiasm and curiosity? Lori Desautels imagines and brings to life just that; discussing the powerful impact and philosophy that "service" and "compassionate presence" germinate in this time of educational and global reform and change. Lori clearly defines educational service and models this concept throughout the book in a way that brings to life the courage, authenticity, and simplicity of marrying the rigor of the academic world to the personal narratives, reflections, and characters that matter most in this time of educating and leading from a strength of heart and the creative intellect of the mind.

~ Minnietta M. Millard, Educator, M.R.E
Boston University School of Theology
and Stained Glass Artist

HOW MAY I SERVE YOU?

Revelations in Education

Lori L. Desautels

Revelations in Education

Printed in the United States of America.

For information:
Revelations in Education
Indianapolis, IN
www.revelationineducation.com

Library of Congress Cataloging-in-Publication Data

Desautels, Lori L.

How May I Serve You?/ Lori L. Desautels

Library of Congress Control Number: 2012930900

p. cm.

ISBN 10: 146995818X
ISBN 13: 9781469958187

Where you place your eyes is what you will always see.

Table of Contents

Gratitudes and Dedication

This story is dedicated to Minnietta M. Millard, my eternal friend and mentor, who changed the world with her visions, advocacy, open heart and brilliant mind, understanding that to live life passionately and fully, fear must be put in its place, inside the illusion of what life is not! On September 9, 2011, Minnietta transitioned into eternal life, where her physical pains have vanished and her wings of *compassionate presence* flutter inside my life in all moments.

This story has taken place inside my mind and heart for many years, and through the knowledge and experiences shared by students, colleagues and family, these notions and narratives have created a story that I hope will encourage educators to not only teach from their hearts, but to lead with their hearts and creative minds.

I want to start by thanking my husband, Michael Desautels, who understands my restless energy and drive to learn and expand. He has lovingly supported our family and provided the time and space for my research, writing, and days of rethinking, pondering and playing with this manuscript.

My heartfelt gratitude to Dr. Lindan Hill for supporting and affirming the time, discussions and reflections as this book was being written. Sitting in his office and discussing the educational philosophies that ground *How May I Serve You?* will never be forgotten.

I want to thank Tom Hakim, Brea Thomas, Jeff Truelock, Walter Nordstrom, Candace Kissinger, and Torrisa Hoffman for sharing your insights, stories and talents as you sit beside your students each day.

Thank you to Joel Thomas for sharing your students' poetry and creating an open mike poetry night in downtown Indianapolis—an experience never to be forgotten by your students.

I want to thank Nellie Stout from the bottom of my heart for her endless time, energy and work on getting this cover, interior and overall book ready to go! Nellie is an artist with a business mind, which lends to a beautiful marriage of creative marketing design, media management and marketing consultation. She has over a decade of corporate, small business and agency experience. Nellie holds a Bachelor of Science degree from Indiana University. Her passion in business is working with entrepreneurs to leverage technology and design to create a unique presence in the marketplace.

I want to thank Lena Reifinger for all her hard work, photo shoots and dedication in creating a cover that speaks to the heart of so many of our students who are struggling and challenged, yet hold a spark of hope and optimism for the future. Lena is a sophomore at Indiana University studying studio art and design, with hopes of eventually working in the design field. Her passions change frequently, sometimes daily, and for now she is enjoying learning about design, her creative talents, and enjoying some self-reflection intermingled with her undergraduate studies. Lena was passionate, reliable and always happily available for the photo shoots for the cover image of the book.

I want to thank Anita Rekher, editor and friend, who never gave up on her belief in this manuscript and in the power of perspective and heart which leads to transformative education. She has been an invaluable support as I attempted to find the perfect publisher for this book.

I want to thank my forever friends, Chris Cherwien and Vicki Mack, who were always excited about every single aspect of this book and its journey, never tiring of my one-dimensional conversations; and if they did, they never showed it.

I will always carry great gratitude and respect for Cindy Farren, my dear friend and colleague who walked the last year and a half with me as we managed our course work, created workshops and events while endlessly discussing how *Service and Heart Leadership* reign at the top of educational reform.

This book is dedicated to all those teachers who listen to their hearts, teach from this place of innate wisdom, and serve the other in extravagant ways.

This book is dedicated to Andrew, my greatest teacher. He keeps life real and tests my patience, accountability, and intuitive gifts, and reminds me to not "play teacher." His sensitivity and authenticity are gifts that are irreplaceable.

This book is dedicated to Sarah, who encourages me to view the wholeness and beauty of each person in this world, transcending the outer layers which sometimes are not so relationally pleasant or true.

This book is dedicated to Regan, who is the free and loving spirit of every child in this world. She churns the imagination and lets go of what she can see with only her eyes.

This book is dedicated to Sam, who quietly lives in the space between child and adult. He reminds me to nourish the quiet and gentle nature of all persons, young and old.

This book is dedicated to Spencer ("Bubby"), who learns in extraordinary ways and requires the imaginative leadership of all his teachers to ignite his passions and gifts, of which there are many.

This book is dedicated to Mr. Thomas and all those students in his class who wrote from their hearts, sharing their poetry with courageous passion. Their poems are found at the end of the book.

This book is dedicated to Mr. Pickett. He taught from the heart and connected with one young man who will never forget his compassion and desire to serve another.

Prologue

Make Your Mark Heavy and Dark

On a recent Friday afternoon, an unemployed twenty year old posted a message on YouTube, simply offering to "be there" for anyone who needed to talk. "I never met you, but I do care," he said.

By the end of the weekend, he had received more than five thousand calls and text messages from strangers taking him up on his offer.

(Retold by Dr. Howard Cutler and The Dalai Lama, from The Art of Happiness in a Troubled World.*)*

What kind of mark do we leave on our students, our children and our own lives? Do we value the entertainment and professional sports industry to the degree of insanity, paying twenty to thirty times the income of that of an effective, caring and creative educator's salary? How do our children and young adults perceive this societal and cultural truth? Do we truly value education in a way that we are willing to reassess, explore, question and discuss a novel and philosophical perspective buried at the root of teaching and learning that shifts the way we prioritize, view and act upon the present dysfunctional educational system? If students are not learning, then education is not happening, and as Sir Ken Robinson clearly states in his revised tenth anniversary edition *Out of Our Minds*, we need to clarify and redefine the purpose of education, and this begins with personalizing it. We can't afford not to!

There are three themes that run throughout this book. These themes do not provide answers, solutions or suggestions for expedient and radical changes, but they do invite the reader to explore the roots of a system that is crying out for changes at a macro and micro level of functioning.

1. How do the personal and collective perspectives of educators, parents and students affect their happiness, success and motivation in school and in life? Do we hold a victim perspective in which experiences, actions and words just occur without our conscious or subconscious participation, or do we hold a perspective that embraces self-design and co-creation?

2. Questions: What do you need? How may I serve you? What can I do? Questions fuel our minds with wonder and options, and they are vehicles for creative solutions and critical thinking skills. When we ask another what he or she needs or desires, we open doors of resistance as defense mechanisms break down and begin to fall away. Building relationships through inquiry, while sustaining them with a steadfast "trust," not only deepens learning, but creates a safe place for self-expression and exploration.

3. Story-telling, personal and communal, has the power to affect the way we ingest, understand and manipulate information and experiences. I once read that there are no new stories or ideas, just new ways of presenting these reoccurring themes and tales. When we listen to another's storyline, we may embrace an epiphany, an insight that we have long awaited inside our own lives. It just may be that word, expression, paragraph or restated theme that strikes a chord in our minds and hearts, changing the way we walk through this world.

Although these themes do not provide answers to the questions posed, my hope in sharing personal narratives, inquiry, and research, based on perspectives, positive psychology and the process of happiness, is to engage the reader in exploring positive shifts that begin inside one heart, one mind and one individual at a time. This is where the trajectory of educational reform begins and ends.

As educators and parents, have we become so concerned about effective instruction, accountability, teacher evaluation, higher and competitive test scores, global economic rivalry, and college acceptance that the joy of teaching and learning has been severed from the creative equation and process of teaching and learning? As parents and educators, are we feeling stressed to the point of exhaustion, apathy and indifference with changes that feel out of our control? Open up and look inside. Look inside your own heart at the perspectives that keep you churning uncomfortably, wearingly or happily inside a pool of emotions and thoughts. *Make your mark heavy and dark…*

You can never cross the ocean unless you have the courage to lose sight of the shore.

~ *Christopher Columbus*

Introduction

Teachers change lives! For better or worse, their presence with students affects change. School environments, administrative policies, and content expertise do not hold a candle to the gentle "personal philosophy" that radiates from teachers who create connections and relationships with their students. Techniques, strategies, and methodologies are important, but we must begin with a compassionate philosophy, an educational spirituality, as the building block for securing happy, effective, and creative students, teachers, and parents. This philosophy must be discussed and shared because as simple as it is, we have forgotten the power of a compassionate presence. Compassion discussed, revered and implemented is the warm conversation we must return to. It is a conversation that must become solution oriented rather than problem oriented, which takes incredible awareness, reflection, and a shift in attitude. Spirituality and education? Be wary of linking the two together, because we are a nation and world that appears to stress competition, growing global economies and mastery of curriculum interspersed with rigor and assessment, assessment, and more assessment.

Read the newspapers, technology links, and headlines. Don't discuss the communion of education and spirituality unless you are referring to parochial or private school culture. This is *public education*, paradoxically, an entity that is starving for a compassionate unity of function, but emphasizes assessment, higher test scores and turn around programs to the detriment of addressing the social and emotional needs of every child and adolescent.

Why would we need a spiritual, compassionate educational foundation? Let me ask you a question. How would you like to "feel felt?" "Feeling Felt" is a term coined by Dr. Dan Seigel, psychiatrist, author and advocate for "mindful awareness," a strategy implemented to focus attention and awareness in everyday experiences. *Feeling felt* is what we all yearn for at the core of our being. Students who "feel felt" begin to feel successful and capable, demonstrating improvement on test scores, self-regulation and levels of motivation. They are able to apply their latent potential and prior knowledge in and outside of school, complying with rules and regulations even though they disagree.

Do you feel felt? Do you feel understood by those you deem important and significant in your life? This concept and quality of character development in its finest moment rests at the core of educational reform. Yet, "feeling felt" is initiated when we learn to take care of ourselves; when we nourish our bodies with adequate sleep, nutritious food, and exercise. We begin to fill our minds with positive thoughts, creative options, and a bit more hope. Often times, this is not easy when we are sitting in the habitual trenches of family and educational upheaval and change. Yet, when we practice listening to that intuitive inner teacher, the heart, we strengthen and multiply our creative alternatives and choices for problem-solving. Creative visualization and quiet reflection literally change our experiences, thoughts and words when we are receptive to the possibilities.

We can ill afford not to begin with this philosophy of compassionate presence, because the research is exploding with findings and studies that the brain is wired for relationships, and that positive emotion and optimism, coupled with feelings of self-worth and success, initiate motivation and drive learning, retention and retrieval of knowledge to new heights. The desire to feel successful deepens learning and is the emotional prerequisite for applicable intelligence and a process for happiness, intimately addressing the emotional and social aspects of education.

Today as I desired nothing more than to write the final words of this manuscript, I received an invitation from a graduate student who asked me to have a sushi lunch and talk about our school years. As the green tea was poured, she looked at me, hesitated and said, "Lori, it has been a tough few weeks, and I want to tell you what has happened." Candace squirmed a bit, played with her chopsticks, and then began to share this story.

Javier's Story

Javier became my student in mid-November after being kicked out of his large high school for absences. It did not take long for me to understand the reason Javier was absent so much from his previous school—he was reading at a fourth grade level and had already been retained three times in his life, making him 16 years old in the 9th grade. Javier avoided school because he did not feel successful, but that changed once we started working together. Javier began to come to school regularly, worked hard in school without any behavior problems, and even happily attended Saturday tutoring to get additional help. Although Javier showed tremendous progress with me and an intense desire to learn, his progress was not fast enough for my school principal, who decided immediately after winter break that it was time for Javier to find a new school. The school I worked at had just opened, and my principal was concerned that Javier would bring our End-Of-Course Assessment scores down.

I did not fully understand the resoluteness of my principal's words until four weeks later, when my principal suspended Javier for three days for wearing black shoes instead of the required white, on an afternoon when I was out of the building. Upon returning to school, I learned of the incident and was extremely upset since the typical punishment for dress code violations was an after-school detention. When I inquired about this unusual disciplinary action, my principal again reiterated that it was time for Javier to find a new school.

Javier and his mother were required to meet with the principal prior to his being allowed back into school after his three-day suspension. Javier's mother asked me to come with them to the meeting because I had established a strong and trusting relationship with the family. While being forced to wait for thirty minutes before the principal would meet with us, the three of us watched as five children walked through the office wearing black shoes!

Once the meeting began, my principal opened the meeting by telling Javier how far behind he was academically compared to his peers and that it was time for him to find a new school. Javier and his mother explained that this was the school they wanted, so my principal shifted back to the issue of the black shoes. Javier explained that he and his mother had been evicted the day he was suspended and had been homeless for the past three days. His mother would not have enough money to purchase him shoes for two weeks, so he wondered if he could wear the black shoes until that time. My principal forcefully said, "No. He needs to have the shoes today or he is being kicked out." I offered to purchase Javier a pair of white shoes in order for him to remain at school, but his mother turned to me and said in Spanish, "It is not about the shoes. The principal no longer wants my son here. It is time for us to find a new place to go." With those words, Javier was gone from school and my life.

Statistically, there is little chance now for Javier to ever graduate from high school. He is currently homeless, Latino, speaks English as a second language, has been raised in a single-parent home, and has been retained already three times in his life. With such ease, my principal traded Javier's future for one less "fail" on the standardized test at the end of the year. As a teacher, this experience makes me wonder what the goal of education has become. When I chose education as a career, it was to work with the tough cases like Javier in order to change my students' life trajectories, not to allow them to become another sad statistic.

Shared by Candace Kissinger
ESL Teacher, Indianapolis, IN

Following Candace's story, I just sat there. I couldn't find any words to describe how I was feeling, or more honestly, what Javier and his mother must have experienced and felt. I share this story because no matter the grade level, age or gathered experiences from teachers and students, educators must embrace and integrate the emotional standard of compassion, extending to our parents and students the power of "feeling felt." Compassion is defined as "a combination of feeling for someone else, experiencing the suffering and a positive move to reduce the suffering of others." Are we truly compassionate with one another? Do we extend to one another even a small invitation to see and express what is possible and all that is going well? As parents and educators, we must begin to implement this emotional support that drives all that we are and do in and out of school.

I cannot type fast enough as I almost feel desperate to share these words, because students like Javier comprise the intellect, the emotional intelligence and heart to be successful, to contribute to another's well-being and to exercise their innate intelligent birthright. However, administrators and teachers hold the power to nurture or kill it off. I am grateful for Candace's presence in Javier's life, and it is my hope that a part of him will remember all that is possible, and what this special teacher saw and nurtured inside him.

One final thought comes to mind focusing on teacher effectiveness, learning outcomes and student growth. It has been brought to my attention and to the attention of educators across the country that the future platforms for assessment of teachers that state and national political and educational reformers will be putting into place will qualify and quantify student growth based on standardized test scores in each classroom and school. This is precisely the reason that the aforementioned administration at Javier's school wanted him out. Candace is one of the most effective educators I have known, creating relationships, building a sense of self-esteem and incrementally raising academic achievement, but her students still fall far behind. She is challenged with a diverse culture of children and adolescents who do not fit into the western world's educational factory model of instruction and assessment. I realize there is not a perfected measurement for our diverse, dynamic and vulnerable learners, but how can we implement such ineffective, short-sighted instruments knowing all that we do about our nation's growing and rich cultural diversity?

Overactive Testing of Today's Students
Brea Thomas

Your palms are sweaty. You can feel your lungs, which are typically the most anonymous aspects of your body. Your eyes turn blurry. Tears? Sweat drops? You aren't sure which. And your stomach is making the most humiliating noises. You have to use the bathroom, you now realize, and it is too late. You were too busy willing your mind to remember miscellaneous items of importance: two No. 2 pencils, a calculator, your registration confirmation, your most comfortable clothes, and oh yes… your mind, which is an endless stream of equations, vocabulary terms, and self-doubting remarks. Your saving grace? That you did remember to eat breakfast!

You were too busy, and now—ten minutes before the test begins—you want to scream out into the silence of the forsaken testing room that has you captive for the next four hours. You slip a piece of gum into your mouth and try to breathe. Those unfamiliar objects in your chest—your lungs—wince in pain and constriction. You start to recall your testing strategies: deep meditative breathing, counting to ten, thinking of a calm and peaceful place.

All of that works… until the proctor brings your exam booklet. You are assigned seat number 17 in a room full of 50 chairs. The proctor writes pertinent information on the board that seems blurry to you. You are supposed to have glasses, but you loathe the feeling of anything on your face. You wish that you had taken some Advil. But it is too late for that because the booklet has arrived and is in front of you, staring at you with its formality. You muster the energy to complete the registration page full of circles to bubble in about everything except your heart rate, and then the… "DO NOT OPEN UNTIL INSTRUCTED" label makes you wince, as you realize that the test in front of you must be endured. It is time to begin.

This is the young adult version of test anxiety. I can recall nausea as early as five days before a test. Sleeplessness. Incessant studying. Fear of failure. Fear of the room. Fear of forgetting. Sleeping with note cards. Sleeping on top of test booklets. GRE madness. *And this was as a young adult.*

Now, reread the aforementioned and place yourself in a six-year-old body. A ten-year-old body. A fifteen-year-old body. You lack the words to articulate exactly how you are feeling.

Today, as I remind my junior students about the PSAT and attempt to distribute preparatory test booklets, hands flail and mouths moan. When I attempt to do practice questions during class, or assign reading comprehension passages—timed—with small incentives like candy on their desks for completion, eyes still roll. iPods are conspicuously retrieved from book bags and slid into one, or both, ears. I then proceed to do the "tap" game: tap, tap Student A on the shoulder, followed by, "Put that away. You cannot listen to that right now" statements. In the increasing "Age of Examinations"—when all schools, students, and teachers are being hyper-measured by assessments—one cannot but wince at where we've arrived, and where we are heading if there is no intervention. Indeed, my eyes are now rolling, too.

It is no secret that today's high school students are faced with the throes of several standardized tests, which occur multiple times per year. Additionally, teachers are required to use pre and post-tests in their daily curriculum, furthering the volume of tests that are filling desks and grade books. For the typical student, test anxiety is weekly. Monthly. And scores are posted online in grade books, or in web portals, with a few paper reports delivered to their houses with "Pass," "Fail," and other designations. Our students are disconnected from their actual scores, and ultimately, from the severity of test scoring. The reality sets in only when scholarships or graduation are at stake. Teachers are left speaking "old news" or "irrelevant news" about testing and what it means for the future.

Yet despite all of the apathy and anxiety, we educators are piling more tests onto our students' desks. And yet their scores are not improving, nor is their morale. Our schools and teachers are being reprimanded, and now May is not even a solid month of teaching—it is "Test Month." Our administrators have to make announcements about "testing etiquette": get rest, eat breakfast, no loud music in the hallways, be on time to school so that you can pass your examination. And most importantly, don't just take a test booklet and Scantron; write your name on them, and refuse to mark anything. Such is the advice to our young minds who hold "testing" just higher than... I am not quite sure what to say here?

My first year as an AP teacher, I learned the hard way that low testing morale exists at all academic levels. Many AP students were simply paying eighty-five dollars for the registration fee, and then refusing to answer any questions—simply to "skip-out" on their final examinations in the AP class. That a student would waste— because there is no other word for it—his or her parents' money, and then sit through the examination period without answering a single question, and not feel guilty about this lackluster behavior, made me ill. This kind of behavior is deplorable.

What or who is to blame for the increasing "test apathy" that even our top students face, in combination with the increasing "test anxiety," disregards the significance of testing.

As teacher and proctor of today's schools, you feel as though you are delivering the stress unto them, hoping the result is they become more cavalier, more self-assured, and more proficient. Ready for the next test. Ready to meet all of the state's mandated requirements. But then, you do not see the students' readiness. Their application of the skills that you've honed all semester plummet when they are tested. You feel their apathy, and if you are an apathetic teacher—you absorb it, too. There is a complete dismantling of education occurring right now, in the area of testing.

The truth is, we are placing our students and educators in a conundrum: prepare for, study for, produce for… the next exam. Also, increase your scores and should you not pass—redo in multiple sessions of remediation. Your teacher may or may not be placed on probation, and you may or may not attend graduation.

As a high school teacher, I see the various sides of the debate quite clearly. Standards are needed, and with them comes assessment—otherwise, differentiation occurs to a degree of unrecognizable CORE standards. I get it. But as Joshua* (name changed for privacy purposes) sits there for the fourth ECA remediation session with furrowed brows and a sweaty forehead, I feel at a loss for the thousands of students who—like Joshua—simply become stumped by the testing scenario.

During practice sessions on Tuesdays and Thursdays, Joshua would glance at me, glance at the booklet, and both of us—in that awkward moment of frustration and confusion—felt stumped. Joshua had me as his English teacher, and despite class instruction on thesis statements, the research process, and multiple selections of reading comprehension, when faced with a new booklet and a too-sharpened pencil, he starts to "clam up" and "freeze." I feel as though those words capture the state of testing in today's school systems; we are clamming up, freezing our students' success in the name of standards that are not truly measuring anything much with accuracy.

What Are the Options?

Could teacher effectiveness highlighting student growth be measured with **Individual Learning Plans** developed by educators, students and parents showing the projects, assessments, discussions, and student performance incurred through a school year? If these assessment measures embedding common core standards sound impossible to you, I think we could all use some minor chest pains these days. We will need to experience some discomfort, angst, and confusion as we create a *compassionate presence* inside our schools, homes and businesses. It is not impossible, it will just take some time, patience, and a collaborative effort to shift perspective, recreating what we know is not working and what we know to be true.

There is good news in the world of educational reform because there are teachers, administrators, students, and parents who care. They care deeply and are creating positive "personal" experiences and classrooms where students feel secure and are encouraged to discover their passions. Inside these classrooms, students embrace their innate genius, upholding mistakes as their greatest learning tools. This is not a book about shoveling schools out from beneath a pile of dysfunction and centralized chaos—or platitudes filled with all that is wrong or erroneous and leaving it at that. There is a burgeoning and heightened awareness of the many challenges our schools face, and when this awareness is activated, change is inevitable.

Educational reform is the talk of the nation as I write these words. Listening to educators, administrators, parents, professors, politicians and students, I'm struck by the similarities and bevy of desires for improvement within the system. Sadly, the means of acquiring these improvements are disillusioning and contradictory. Driving home from classes at the university this week, I was struck by the contrast of flickering stars across the vast nighttime sky, the waning moon, and fat flakes of snow, while listening to National Public Radio. The round table bantering gathered the notions and arguments of deans of education, school administrators, and political leaders arguing the facets of change that must be implemented inside schools to garner higher achievement, mastery of learning and competitive national educational test scores. I'm reminded that there is no amount of resources, turnaround programs placed inside "so-called failing schools," nor state mandated eight-step action plans that will fix a dysfunctional system that is crying out for enduring change. Fixing a problem, person, or school is an integral part of the dilemma.

When we keep *doing, never stopping to listen to the wisdom of our intuitive organ, the heart, or to the words of one another,* we spin in suffocating circles of negative emotion, because what we all crave in the end is to feel successful, to feel we have made a difference, and to feel worthy of what is before us. The only lasting way to attain these feelings of self-worth individually and systemically comes from within, where the power and magnitude of heartfelt compassion reigns. When we see and imagine the best in one another, we begin to posit those feelings, experiencing improvement across all facets of our lives. Optimism is contagious. Perspective drives learning, teaching, and **life**, and we must return to the power of playing with "perspective" as we enter into this conceptual age of educational reform and expansion.

We've been studying and researching various opposing opinions, methodologies and mandates from a national transition-to-teaching program, Teach for America, comparing and contrasting its premises to the intelligent and forthright writings from former educator and New York state "teacher of the year" John Taylor Gatto. The two viewpoints and approaches appear quite opposite in structure and function, but their focus on growing emotional, social and academic achievement, coupled with their desire to improve our educational system, may run parallel.

I am currently one of the instructors for the Teach for America graduate students who are first and second year teachers in Indianapolis, Indiana, a Midwest sanction of this national transition-to-teaching program. I'm struggling a bit with this organization's seemingly compulsory flavor of teaching methodology and mind set for approaching and affecting national change within our public schools. I also believe strongly in self-directed and experiential learning, the collaborative method John Taylor Gatto describes as the *congregational principle*, from his book *Dumbing Us Down*. I believe as a culture, we have been conditioned by many factors to be extremists in our words, thoughts and behaviors. We also have become conditioned and impatient unless a short term solution is visible and at hand. When we collectively hold a reverence for absolutes, we miss out.

I believe Mr. Gatto and Teach for America could benefit from a philosophy embracing a balanced perspective of instructional rigor, feedback from assessments, and a reflection of how the assessment results inform instruction in all areas of a child's development. We begin to forfeit the force that drives every individual to feel better and successful—*compassion*. Compassion is defined as an awareness of one's struggle or suffering and a desire to assist in alleviating the suffering. When we assist another, we also benefit by broadening and changing our perspectives, attitudes and the fluid flow of positive emotion and thought.

All children are born with an excitement to explore, create, and interact. We are relational beings. Research reports that establishing and maintaining healthy relationships drives our intrinsic motivation to feel optimistic and secure and increases positive emotion, especially during perceived stressful events. Most children enter pre-school and kindergarten with enthusiasm and a curiosity to play and imagine, while gradually defining who they are through connecting with other children, teachers and adults. Somehow, this innocent and irreplaceable enthusiasm seems to vanish at early ages. Why?

We live in a time when political and educational reformers around the country and within individual states are continually developing, reinventing, and rewrapping core content standards for teaching the subject areas of language arts, math, science and social studies. I believe we have reached a point where we must stop doing and rethink the philosophical foundation upon which these educational standards, benchmarks, and core assessments are founded.

Below are questions that must be considered before we move forward. Are students happy in school? Do they feel secure and safe; secure enough to make mistakes, learning from the projects, tests, and often times lowered marks? Do they feel stimulated by the instruction and content? Are they curious? Do they feel purpose and relevancy when standards and subjects are presented? Do they feel successful? How important is it for students to feel successful knowing they spend 12,000 hours plus inside classrooms and schools through a span of 12 or more years of academic preparation? Are we providing the guidance and listening skills for students to move to the heart during challenging times? Does acquiring higher test scores in math and science equate to personal fulfillment? Were the inventors of Under Armor, Google, and Disney World successful because of their high math and science scores? Teaching a child *how* to problem solve, *how* to critically think, and *how* to get along with others, while seeing diversity as a gift rather than an obstacle to penetrate, is part of this global conversation. Do we stress in schools our commonalities as humans, or are we subconsciously or consciously focused on our differences?

When 18-year-olds enter college, the work force, or trade schools, how many of them are asking questions like, "How do I find meaning in my life?" "What is my purpose?" How many young adults are living in the present moment with no idea of how to plan for a future? How many adolescents live for Friday night? It has been my experience as a teacher, mother, instructor in higher education and school counselor that many of our young adults are pondering these life-forming questions. We need to listen to them. When my 19-year-old son is restless, ornery and struggling, his grades in school drop, he loses things, and he's irritable. When he's taking care of "business," his grades in school improve! For me, his grades are a barometer for managing life, yet this doesn't equate to self-fulfillment or personal happiness. As educators and parents, we begin listening with a five-word question that initiates the "conversation." *How may I serve you?*

If world peace is truly a global desire and all individuals begin life inside the arena of a learning and teaching culture, then as educators, parents, and community members, we must become responsible for mentoring the emotional and social needs of our future world citizens. Mentoring is not spoon-feeding information and academic content into the mouths of our students, because that knowledge may be irrelevant within a few years. We listen, we inquire, and then we gently guide them to their expressed or demonstrated passions and strengths through a dialogue of inquiry and creative design. We begin to model self-initiated instruction in which children and adolescents remember and build upon their innate strengths and interests. We guide our students in creating purposeful experiences in and out of schools, coupled with a flow of ideas that never dry up.

How do we begin to delve inside these notions, recreating an educational system that emphasizes compassion? I believe lasting change will occur when we begin from the bottom up, small incremental shifts that focus on one student, classroom and school at a time. We begin to focus on what is going well and what is going right. If we are to effect change, then turn around schools guided by effective leadership, start with a *compassion-driven perspective, incorporating emotional and social engagement.* It begins with a leadership that is patient in taking an inventory of all aspects of the school's culture, diversity and needs. This inventory informs discussions. Conversations are initiated exploring the holistic needs of educators, parents and students. A compassion-driven curriculum is neither trite nor fluffy. It is educational rigor at its finest and best practice for all.

At an early age, children do not recognize color, race, status, diversity or ethnicity in a negative or competitive light. They accept what is before them with a hearty appetite to *learn and discover.* We know that through the early processes of familial and societal conditioning, a child's values, beliefs and culture are formed. These formed belief systems often create the divisions and stereo typing of people in later years, clearly erasing much of the naïve and loving nature of that which is innate to all children in this world.

Research presents a novel view and understanding of human development that exceeds our genetic composition. We now understand that genetic inheritance is half the equation, as the environment's role in our overall cognitive, emotional and social development matters greatly. The enrichment of that environment or lack thereof affects the major emotional, cognitive and social functioning systems of each individual. Gene expression is not limited, and the potential for growth and expansion inside our lives is enormous. As educators and parents, we are privileged to understand how significant an enriched environment can positively affect our child and adolescent's development and experiences in life.

Here is where the critical conversation must commence. Are we able to create a balance of assessment-driven mastery examining student performance and growth? Are we paying attention to the sub skills and academic nuances as we examine the strengths and challenges of the learning profiles of each student? To be compassionate is to be creative, innovative, and open to how we address each student's culture, circumstances and experiences impacting their hours, behaviors and engagement in the classroom.

National Core Standard—Compassionate Curriculum

A compassionate curriculum will be explored and discussed in three parts. First and foremost, we must ask one another what we need. *How may I serve you?* When we do not understand the needs and thoughts of one another, tempers flare, agitation brews, and we lose sight of the aptitudes, skills, and gifts each of us contributes to this educational cauldron of diversity. Secondly, we must listen where understanding another's mind and heart is activated. We listen in a space where we do not listen to respond, but listen to understand. The third component of a compassionate curriculum is "self-reflection coupled with creative design." When we understand the needs of our students, parents, children and colleagues, we can begin to create meaningful and relevant subject matter, experiences, and opportunities that germinate a desire to be invested in this educational process.

Now we must include the most significant interpersonal skill that all people need when creatively relating to one another—*empathy*. When we empathize with our students, colleagues, and parents, we intuitively open our eyes to a perspective that might not have been discovered or understood before asking the question, "What do you need? How may I serve you?" Next, at a distinct interpersonal depth, we listen beneath behaviors and even words. Listening for direction and feedback, we are able to design ways to stay emotionally connected with increased understanding. This is the place where education begins and ends. When we guide our students to reach "within," to the heart, we inadvertently discover *our* passions, aptitudes and strengths as well. Old habits die hard, and it is only through practice and repetition that innovative ways of relating to one another, along with new experiences, become permanent.

Before you read another page, try this little experiment. If you have found yourself struggling with someone—a family member, business partner, co-worker, etc.—feeling agitated, annoyed, or misunderstood, approach the person and the situation in a novel way, with an intention to ask and listen: How can I make this easier for you? What do you need? How can I help? Then observe. Observe the angst, anger and frustration gradually slip away as the question is posed and received with a bit of surprise, sincerity and authenticity. This is where the magic of discovering empathy for another begins to open pathways of understanding and creative exploration. The processes of learning and teaching are now present and activated as cooperative and collaborative components, where broadened perspectives drive compassion and ultimately breed exceptional teaching and learning.

Isn't it time to place angry and agitated nationalism, separatism, world wars, exorbitant military spending, and an intense intolerance of one another into a locked box? Isn't the classroom the place where emotional and social skills are nurtured, diversity discussed, and dialogues begun? This worn-out container of conflicted notions holds the old stories of pedagogy and political baggage no longer applicable in this world brimming with possibility of global communication and collaboration. There is no greater time for implementing creative service to one another, embracing a conversation that holds compassion in high esteem and a national standard that will enhance the acquisition of educational content and skills needed in this ever-changing world.

I am excited for the day when my children and grandchildren will be video conferencing with students from Japan, India and China who together will create a communication and performance based assessment that will align our countries with a deepened respect for the rich diversity each holds, rather than worrying and placing competitive edges inside the hearts and souls of those who were born to relate, to inquire and wonder!

We now begin…

Offering
This work I do is an offering
from my hand and heart.
Let the imagination awaken the power that
is within each student, releasing healing communion throughout the world.

~Shelley Richardson

Part One

Questions

Who was your favorite teacher? What did he look like? What did she wear? What look on his face bothered you? How did she walk? Who was your least favorite teacher? Did you promise yourself you would someday return to that teacher, allowing him or her to see just who you became?

Teachers have the power to change the course of a life, to build or to destroy. Sound dramatic? Research shares that by the time a student graduates from high school he or she has spent over 12,000 hours in a school environment. Yet there appears to be a lack of coursework mentoring educators in addressing the power and magnitude of teaching from the extravagant combination of heart and mind. Maybe there is an overall misunderstanding from political and educational reformers addressing this core component. Why? If we understand the significance of *positive relationships* within the context of life and educational practices, the process must be explored and discussed. Education networks through all professions and stages of human life. Much like the development of a child or adolescent, schools and educators pass through developmental stages mimicking their cultures, societal directives and personal belief systems.

Questions are an integral aspect of change. We often view questions with skepticism because we tend to assume an answer is needed, or the experts posing such questions are unsure of a solution. I believe questions and inquiry are healthy aspects of critical thinking and problem solving enterprises. Skilled questioning is sorely missing inside educational reform in the United States. Implementing inquiry alleviates the inertia of learning felt by so many students and educators. The power of questions can initiate the formation of positive perspectives in classrooms and schools that are awaiting discovery, action and expansion.

I challenge the reader with some significant questions throughout this book addressing educational and therefore societal reform. If we are to inaugurate momentous and lasting changes inside the present educational system, do we not begin with a compassionate philosophy of change? I am speaking about a philosophy in which our collective perspectives and beliefs initiate a type of   leadership that listens deeply, empowering and modeling for its followers traits of social and emotional equity, a partnership built on equity, grounded in collaboration.

Are we finally ready for a house made of bricks rather than temporary homes constructed of sticks and straw? A house where special interests, power, control and the continual implementation of one-dimensional standardized assessments are left at the entrance? I believe it is time to take a look at who we are inside this highly evolving and expanding world of digital and creative possibility. Have politicians at state and national levels, alongside businesses eager to open charter schools, forgotten and forfeited the hearts and souls of many parents, teachers and students?

To understand where we are going, we must take a long look at where we have been. Over the past century and a half, schools have emphasized two areas of intelligence: language and mathematics. We now know through the research of Multiple Intelligences, defined by developmental psychologist Dr. Howard Gardner from Harvard University, that there are eight to nine areas of intelligence that are identified with specific physical regions in the brain. Yet we as a society are forced to teach these core standards and toggle the evident achievement gaps and low test scores by creating assessments that continually call for one right answer or solution. Educator John Gatto Taylor writes, "After an adult life-time spent teaching school, I believe the method of mass schooling is its only real content. Don't be fooled into thinking that good schools, good curriculum or good teachers are the critical determinants of our children's education. All the lessons of school prevent children from keeping appointments with themselves and with their families to learn lessons, in self-motivation, perseverance, self-reliance, courage, dignity and love—and lessons in service to others."[1]

The public education system in the United States has one of the lowest graduation rates in the world, with math and science scores stagnant or dropping. This is not new information, as a floundering educational system has been highlighted in the media spotlight for the last several years. As a nation, how are we rectifying and promoting **lasting** positive movements in student growth and teacher effectiveness within our schools? I believe assessment measures and instructional practices viewed as processes, not final outcomes, are beneficial interpretations. When we implement the informed instruction based on these interpretations of sub-skills measured, students will experience incremental success and an understanding of **how** to improve. The emphasis on feedback and self-reflection is paramount when we interpret data tracking academic and behavioral progress.

But are our students learning the compassionate skills to live with one another creatively and authentically? There is no doubt that teacher efficacy is directly correlated to student growth. On a national and state level, I do believe we are taking steps to promote teacher accountability and effectiveness within our schools. However, it feels once again like we are creating short-term measures that are temporary and cyclical as schools follow the economical, political and societal signs of the changing times. Do schools across the world and nation share a teaching philosophy that is one of design and imaginative leadership, in which the well-being and holistic health of the parent, teacher and student are uplifted, protected and revered? I do not believe we are even close to answering this question in an affirmative manner.

We open charter schools while closing ineffective and failing schools. We offer school vouchers, neglecting the fact that many of these private schools are full and have a rigorous process in place for acceptance of any student. We write, read and sell textbooks filled with numbered and highlighted differentiated strategies and techniques, hoping to improve the data results, achievement gaps and academic mastery of our students. The trend of quick fixes and the drive to implement high performance and effective leadership leaves us tired, feeling drained of the emotional energy that was designed to enhance learning and teaching. There is hollowness at the center of the many policies, mandates and programs initiated to promote lasting educational change.

At the very center of this present academic curriculum is a concept that seems to be missing—*a living compassionate curriculum.* When does the change and passion for being inside the process of educational revelation occur? I believe it occurs when we stop doing, and listen to the needs of one another. A lasting change in any dynamic interactive system must have a grass roots beginning. This includes a philosophical foundation to build upon, a philosophy that induces relational learning. We must listen to one another as we move forward, creating a culture that promotes broadened perspectives, opening minds and hearts to the possibilities of collaboration even when there are fiery disagreements.

Who has actually asked the students what they desire or need in this time of educational change? Have we listened to our students as we create and deliver policies, core standards and professional development for teacher and student performance and proficiency? What do they bring to school environments that is not being heard or acknowledged, possibly contributing to a misunderstanding or a disallowance of academic, social and emotional growth? I'm not suggesting that we become student governed, or not create high expectations for our vulnerable and lower performing children and adolescents. It goes without saying that to embrace difficult problems, we must listen deeply. I'm aware that there are classrooms, schools and townships that place a greater priority on student inquiry and discussion. Yet, I would like to hear and see more district and systemic interactions between administration, teachers, parents and students. Sometimes we assume we recognize the needs and desires of those smaller in stature. However, our engaging and multi-faceted students are the contributors of feelings and thoughts inside classrooms where the magic of learning and teaching potential soars to new realms.

Several months ago as I mused over *Time Magazine's* issue, "What Makes a School Great," these words struck me as a paradox: "According to an upcoming McKinsey and Co. study, „just 23% of new teachers in the US come from the top third of their college classes; 47% come from the bottom third. In other words, we hire lots of our lowest performers to teach, and then we scream when our kids don't excel.' " Who truly are these lower performers, these student learners, because research verifies that many schools **only** teach two out of eight to nine intelligences?

Over twenty years ago, Howard Gardner, psychologist, author and Harvard professor, opened our eyes and minds, highlighting various brain regions that directly correlate eight to nine areas of intelligence. If you are not savvy with linguistics, which embraces the spoken and written language, or mathematical-logical reasoning, you quite possibly may not perform well according to standardized tests, which are created and assessed for linguistic and math mastery. In this twenty-first century, we know that multiple intelligences, emotional experiences, prior knowledge and connections are significant factors and contributors to deep learning and higher level thought processes as we reach out to the rich diversity inside our classrooms. I would enjoy the perspective of a talented teacher who possibly struggled with traditional teaching and learning methods, but through his or her experiences, understands the learning challenges of his students, aligning with those who need to move and use their hands when learning. I would appreciate a teacher who understands the significance of music, connecting to the poetic hearts of those children who learn in genius ways through melodies and sounds.

Spencer is 14 years old and in the eighth grade. He is filled with latent talents: musical beats and rhythms, humor, story-telling, athleticism, sensitivity and a growing but clear self-awareness of whom he is, in and out of the class-room. Spencer has some minor learning challenges, but they are only quantifi-able and questionable in the processing of language and fine motor skills from the traditional teaching methods of lecturing, reading independently and indi-vidual worksheets. When he is allowed to express his knowledge through mu-sic, hands-on projects, and experiencing the subject matter by using his body, imagination and personal expression, he transforms into a superior student.

Research has shown that there is over 90% retention over a 24-hour peri-od when students are allowed to teach what they need to learn, and this is ex-actly how I assisted Spencer in studying for a science test a few months ago. We worked through the equations of acceleration and velocity until he had clearly explained each step and process of all the word problems presented. He understood the definitions and talked through each one as we created cards with colored markers and discussed how we discovered the answers and conclu-sions offered from his study guide. He was ready for the test. Spencer received a 61% on his test and in fact was in the top half of the class, as the average score was 45%. Although three quarters of this teacher's students failed, there is rarely reflection, re-teaching of subject matter or an exploration of how this assessment example and sample of failing test scores is a repetitive occurrence in this science lab.

I'm certain this science teacher would benefit from self-reflecting and assessing what is working well and what is creating blockages for the majority of students. Would it be necessary to redesign her curriculum and assessment of student performance, exploring learning styles, emotional connections, and strengths of her students? It is apparent she is not personalizing content while encouraging the development of their innate abilities. I believe that self-esteem and a love of science are potentially being killed off in this classroom environment. We cannot afford to sit back and watch this continue; not because we are statistically and economically falling behind other countries, but because a student's sense of self-worth and self-efficacy is being dangerously questioned and diminished. This teacher is not effecting student growth; she is squelching it.

Would Spencer be considered a low performer in higher education, as *Time Magazine* discussed, if he were to enter into education one day based on traditional educational instruction, content, assessments and standards? Would Spencer possibly be an exceptional teacher to those students and all students who do not learn subject matter well from the traditional factory model teaching methods? Yes, without a doubt. Spencer could be an exceptionally engaging and intuitive teacher, relating to hundreds of students who struggle with formal instruction and traditional educational practices.

Gray Area...Art and Science

I believe teaching is an art and a science, an organic process rich with inquiry coupled with the potential for self-directed learning. Teaching is creating every moment anew. We need to embrace the art and science of this process as we examine assessments and mastery of content, while holding the perspective of an inclusive classroom as a prosperous resource for the diversity within. Here is the place we consciously open our minds and hearts to students, parents and teachers who are doing their best with the experiences, knowledge and beliefs each has accrued through the years.

"Creative Curriculum" is of utmost importance in this conceptual age of the 21st century. Although this question was asked in the introduction of this book, it is worth pondering again. How many students are socially, emotionally and cognitively ready to enter higher education at age 18? Think about this question. Most high school seniors in their second semester are taking classes that do not feel meaningful, and students are not invested in the outcomes of their last semester of high school. Why? Colleges have either accepted the students for enrollment during the fall semester, or students have decided on academic or vocational tracks, making plans following graduation. Many seniors do not think past a week or month and are unsure of how to plan for six to twelve months out. There is a stinging urgency felt by most high school seniors to just "get out."

What is left of high school is an entire semester where most high school seniors in public schools are biding their time, indifferent, unmotivated, skipping half or most of their classes, and are dangerously restless, bored and eager to leave. Think of the student, parent and teacher connections and life preparations we, as an invested community, could encourage and instill in these last five months prior to graduation. I envision a senior year second semester curriculum in which all public schools offer a service internship giving college or vocational credit and recognition for accrued service hours. The families and schools would choose a service organization where students develop resumes, observe, visit, and research, discovering personal value, strengths, interests and purpose inside this service project. These internships would be aligned with a performance based task and assessment presented and showcased prior to graduation.

A "creative service curriculum" not only produces a meaningful and relevant environment, but strokes the emotional and social skills needed to live outside the walls of classrooms and schools. Senior groups led by parent and teacher mentors would collaborate two to three times a week during the spring semester, discussing plans and asking questions while implementing self and group assessments. These assessments, given by educational facilitators, would address and inform academic, emotional and social outcomes, while discovering what is possible beyond tomorrow night or the "weekend rager."

Are we preparing our students for life outside of school? Author and educator Pat Wolfe states, "It is the role of schools to prepare students to live outside of schools." Do we consciously or subconsciously embrace a mindset that feels it must fix, coagulate and secure new leadership, implementing additional teaching training programs, while raising the bar in educator, student and academic preparation? If we begin to meet those aforementioned criteria, are we addressing the heart of education transformation? I don't believe so. Time and time again most of us look outside ourselves to save another soul, trying to improve his or her character, fixing what we perceive to be wrong, etc. We correct the misgivings we see in another by generating solutions or changes that originate from the "outside in" rather than the "inside out." Educationally, we do this by slipping in tighter mandates and higher expectations for educators and students.

The Indianapolis Public Schools have recently reported a significant increase in graduation rates, and the administration has explained that this increase in graduation rates is largely due to the implementation of "graduation coaches" placed in many of the struggling high schools within the city. The intention of incorporating graduation coaches is one of assistance, increasing proficiency and student performance while increasing the number of students who hold and leave school with a diploma. But again, what is the purpose and the larger perspective of incorporating and financing this venture? The graduation coaches' role is to tutor for content mastery, assisting students in passing their courses with higher assessment scores, but following the assessment, graduation, and twelve years of compulsory schooling, what is next? Did we reach the heart and intelligence of this student? Did we allow her to discover her creative aptitudes, while collectively dispensing the tools she will need to self-discover, experience and generate inventive possibilities for her future?

There are always those who thrive educationally when education decline seems to be the order of our nation. There are always those who attain clarity inside environments of confusion. You do not need everyone or anyone else to align with your desire—you only need to align with your desire and intention of well-being! Could this not be a motto for international educational reform?

Pat Wolfe reminds us that content and subject matter will always change. She stresses that the larger concepts and big ideas of critical thinking and problem solving are skill sets we need to address. I agree with these notions, although there is more that can be done. We need to address and assist students in brain-based strategies of "how to monitor their thinking and emotion, enhancing ways we remember and retrieve information through emotional connections presented inside instruction," educator and author Robin Fogarty explains. "Emotions are the gatekeepers of the intellect. Emotional hooks are necessary for long term learning; negative emotions can become blocks to learning. Emotions and learning cannot be separated."

We need a gentle merging of both. Instead of going in and fixing a classroom, or redirecting and re-teaching a student's way of thought, we would all benefit by nurturing and acknowledging "how" our own thoughts create perspectives that may or may not be true for others. Are we able to slide a bit more joy and gratitude into the educational mix even for a moment? It would only take a moment to experience its incredibly powerful effects! When we have the eyes to see ourselves, a child, parent or colleague doing his or her best, we have uplifted ourselves and those around us tenfold in those moments of noticing one positive aspect of a behavior, a gesture or comment.

This is the key ingredient to *educational transformation, broadening perspectives and finding the gift of an experience in every teaching and learning moment.* Compassion for ourselves spawns compassion for others, which is the fuel that ignites changes. Yes, teaching children the big ideas of how to approach a problem by exploring both sides is vitally important, but what about the heart and soul that drive and initiate our thinking? When we desire to rescue a system, teacher or student, we must first move within, to the landscape of our own feelings and thoughts, seeing how compassion is at work in our own lives—or not?

If we are to respond to *Time Magazine* articles and its recent cover story, "What Makes a School Great?" we must look at the dissension, the deep crevices of a systemic thought process that is not functioning up to its potential, because if it were, movies like *Waiting for Superman* would not be created on the basis of a broken and dysfunctional system. There are plenty of educators who are joyfully teaching and learning within a flow of creative energy affirming all those students who walk through their doors. They have the eyes to see what is going well and right, and this begins long before they pull into the school parking lot or administration building. It is initiated when they awaken each morning and fully feel all that is within. They listen to their hearts, those treasures that never lead us astray unless we forget to listen.

Who was your favorite teacher? What did he look like? What did she wear? What look on his face bothered you? How did she walk? Who was your least favorite teacher? Did you promise yourself you would someday return to that teacher, allowing him or her to see just who you became?

A **five-word** question unmistakably opens hearts and perspectives when any conflict, angst or dissension arises in or out of school: *How may I serve you?* Tell me what you need. How can I help you? I believe that the esoteric skills that are critical in connecting and inspiring our students are difficult to quantify and measure. As a society, we are eager for the quick and concrete solution and result, but the results of academic and behavioral assessments inside our schools are reportedly negative and low. We keep raising the behavioral and academic standards, but we are not delving into the root causes of what is stifling the innate potentials of our students and educators. What are the keys that will unlock the hearts and minds of our students, teachers and parents? Look inside a simple question: *How may I serve you?*

Racing for What?

We continually create and develop new teacher programs and degrees for teacher and business leadership. Yet we ignore the power of relationships, service to another, and the fundamental effects of relational learning when we explore relationships within the contextual fabric of education. Maybe we have transitioned into an information and digital technology age, where matters of the heart have been placed aside as we acquire and frantically teach to and for the tests, meet annual yearly progress, and worry incessantly about student achievement.

We can measure heart connections and service to one another but these relational skills take time to unfold, observe and assess. The irony is that the national government is asking the states to **race to the top** in meeting national academic mandates; but as we race along this one-dimensional track, we are not winning. We are creating a collective mass consciousness of competitive, information-driven politicians and administrators who are indirectly or inadvertently asking students and teachers to leave their feelings and hearts out of the equation.

There is no question that teachers and schools need to be held accountable for student growth and teacher effectiveness in mastery of curriculum and delivery, but the attitude is once again antiquated at best, leaving the imagination and creative visions of both teacher and student in the dust. How do we incorporate our common core standards into creative innovations so that educator and student are ingeniously learning within the context of standardized assessment? It is a thought to seriously ponder.

How do we return to a rich holistic curriculum that propagates higher order and creative thought processes? How do we connect to the "whole" child and adolescent so that our deepened understanding positively affects and strengthens their learning? Getting to know the "whole" child, assisting her in contributing her own thoughts and ideas inside the academic equation, could be the root of social, emotional and academic success in and out of school.

Focusing on the **whole** student, differentiating to discover his strengths and passions, is what author and motivational speaker Daniel Pink affirmed in his book *A Whole New Mind*. He describes the magnificent shift inside education and the business world as it moves from an Information Age of linear, logical and computer-like approaches where number two pencils, standardized assessment, and MBA's crunched numbers and cracked codes driving learning, business, and careers of yesterday to what is now evolving into a Conceptual Age. [2] Daniel Pink states, "The future belongs to a very different kind of person with a very different kind of mind—creators, empathizers, pattern recognizers, and meaning makers. These people, artists, inventors, designers, story tellers, caregivers, consolers, and big picture thinkers—will now reap society's richest rewards and share in its greatest joys." [3]

For over one hundred years the western world of education and work force have been grounded in notions of analytical thought and manipulation of information, providing singular mechanistic solutions for most presented challenges. This type of thought and approach worked well in its time, but we have moved to an empathic, relational and meaning driven epoch that is demanding compassion and differentiation in education and inside the world of business **if** we are to survive and thrive in this new global economy.

The college professor encourages the young freshman to keep going. "You can do this; I have seen the determination in your eyes and in your work. Let me know how I can help you."

The second grade teacher looks down. "Kyle, I am sick of this behavior. What are you going to do when no one talks to you or wants to be around you anymore? What is the world going to do with you?"

The seventh grade teacher looks into the eyes of a young man that was just bullied in the halls of a large middle school. "We will work this out. You made a great decision to come to me."

There is one memory most of us share as we grow into our lives, whether we are 13, 20, 40, or 80 years of age. We remember our favorite and /or least favorite teacher, coach or individual in or out of the school environment. When we look back into our years spent inside classrooms or other significant learning environments, we hold these remembrances with negative or positive emotion or maybe just indifference. Were they deemed favorites because of the math, science, and social studies drilled into our heads, or was it because we felt respected, cared for and connected to that teacher or individual? Most often, we will feel gratitude or possibly a distinct positive emotion when thinking of a favorite teacher or coach because he or she took the time and energy to form a connection, building a relationship that inspired us to forge ahead and try… we felt affirmed in our personhood. This teacher more than likely allowed us our journeys, with a gentle guidance and open mind. Maybe they saw the vision, the masterful design of who we could be when we were unaware and stuck in the "what is" of a story that **was not** serving us so well.

Contrast

When I was little, but old enough to converse and ask questions, my nickname was "Last Word Lori." This name spun a trail shadowing me into adulthood, and rightfully so. I am neither proud nor ashamed of this label. It feels authentic and part of who I am, or more accurately, who I am becoming. Whether it was the last word in an argument or a question I felt compelled to ask, desiring a hearty response that felt logical and made sense, was a self-induced mission.

Now research has declared and shared that "questions" are the most important part of the learning process. The brain loves questions and keeps processing them long after they have been asked. Here is where the organic process of life and learning intimately dance—*inside the question.*

This is a story of questions and mystery within the framework of education where all people begin in life. It is the story of the *power of thought and perspective.* Bundles of thoughts circulate in our minds, forming beliefs, and beliefs create perspectives. We collectively label our beliefs as right, wrong, good or bad, but they are just thoughts until we give them meaning and credence. As teachers, administrators and parents, we are responsible for the thoughts and perspectives we hold or evaluate. I encourage you to explore your perspectives, seeing how rigid or pliable they feel, reaching inside while exploring this new paradigm of teaching and learning.

Contrast, exploring opposing events, provided through teaching and life occurrences, is a gift if we choose to experience it that way. When we see what we desire, we give further attention to this person or event, therefore boosting positive emotion. When we are confronted with a situation or person that feels taxing, we can choose how we respond. If we feel angry, just the allowance and acceptance of how we feel assists us in shifting to an improved feeling. We then can begin to carve out a place for an opening heart and mind that embraces thoughts which slowly improve and are increasingly productive and beneficial inside our developing understanding of any situation. We have the freedom to alter our thoughts, responding from a place of understanding, but not necessarily agreeing.

I believe all persons tend to struggle, becoming increasingly frustrated when they find themselves entangled inside another's problems or challenges, which is ultimately the other individual's journey. What looks bothersome to us may be just the perfect in-

cident or circumstance for another student's, parent's, or educator's personal growth and development. I believe the flowing
stream of effective and personalized education requires a malleable perspective, a keen active awareness, but more notably—an
active, compassionate *presence*. Compassion is allowing ourselves to
travel through the twists and turns of life's mysteries, carrying a
deep understanding that each parent, child and educator is doing
his or her best, though it may not look like this from the outside
in.

Education is life. Education is about all of us; who we are, where
we've traveled, where we're going, and how we are evolving.
Schooling is not education. I believe in this time we are schooling our children, not educating them! Haven't we all at one time
or another asked ourselves, What am I doing here? What is my
purpose? Where is life taking me? What is next? How do I reach
my goals? What happened to my dreams? Pat Wolfe's words ring
through my head: "The purpose of school is to live outside of
school" [4]

A classroom is where most of us discovered friends and
learned about rules, lines, and order. Maybe we were affirmed in
even the smallest way that we still remember. And if we were not
affirmed, maybe we can look back and appreciate the pinched and
unkind remarks that we recall years later. We learned about formal
instruction and how math, reading and writing skills were a top
priority inside this structured day; but this wasn't the heart of our
school days. Schools became the place where we explored, questioned and defined who we were in this ever-expanding world of
teachers, students, and strangers while developing an independen-
cy that was challenged with a desire to fit in! We chose perspectives, argued our views, but mostly tried to avoid embarrassment
while creating the personas and masks that would serve us well or
not so well in our young adolescent and adult years. As we developed into young adults, the hours spent away from our homes

increased and the strangers that soon directed our lives and feelings of self-worth became permanent fixtures for nine months a year.

Why speak of this socialization process and emotional development tangled with formal instruction, rules, assignment notebooks, texts and number two pencils? If we do not engage our students, we will have missed getting to know these unique individuals. More importantly, we will have missed out on getting to know ourselves. Research reveals we currently are instructing bored, uninterested and apathetic students who *feel* unsuccessful and demonstrate these feelings through negative words and behaviors. If the academic curriculum does not include an integral component of a *compassionate presence*, we all will experience the adversarial consequences: repetitive circles of trendy and frantic solutions attempting to fix a problem we don't begin to understand.

Imagination

Somewhere in our childhoods many of us acquired the mindset that when you play, imagine, or create inventive strategies to entice and invigorate learning, the content is lost. This is unequivocally false and an untrue assumption. I believe the most rigorous curriculum is one of creative exploration. Test scores have soared across curriculums when students are engaged and feel that learning is not only meaningful in their lives, but fun. Why can't we have fun and be productive and successful? We have become rubric (assessment) dependent educators and students. Yet, there is no rubric when a new teacher sets up and establishes a classroom culture. When the joy returns to the classroom, so too will the creative mind and intuitive genius born and bred in every child.

Happiness…What Does it Have to Do With Education? Everything!!

What is the purpose of education? Why spend time exploring favorite or disfavored teachers and the marks they left behind? We can't afford not to explore what creates happy, peaceful and successful teachers and students. A couple of months ago, I stood in front of a new cohort group, 118 Teach for America first and second-year teachers. Their induction and institute for teaching in the Indianapolis Public Schools took place over the past summer, and as I type these words they have currently spent 16 weeks inside their classrooms searching for ways to connect *content to the learner.* Many of them looked at me as if I had three eyes when I offered "a process for happiness" through building relationships as a remedy for starters. Relational learning is far more important than rigorous assessment and closing the achievement gaps.

Following the first class and presentation, I asked for exit slips, small sheets of paper that asked three questions: What did you come away with? What would you like to explore more of? And what, if any, practical applications did this content provide? The overall desire and request from the class was for tangible strategies, ways to teach and instruct so the subject matter is relevant and meaningful. But there is a question that drives all strategies, techniques, and assessment-driven teaching and learning. *How may I serve you?* When we listen, deeply listen, to a response from this question, we hear the inner voice of that student that informs us, when we take the time to know who we are and who our students are inside—*relational learning!* Students who feel heard and experience security are happier and feel positive about their role in and out of the classrooms.

When people's thoughts are positive, there is a direct correlation to their physical, emotional and social well-being. Our improved health and capabilities in relating to others are enhanced in ways that promote serenity and an understanding of diversity, and more importantly, we feel happier. In the Dalai Lama's new book, *The Art of Happiness in a Troubled World*, his co-author, psychiatrist Dr. Howard Cutler, states, "Cultivating compassion breeds happiness and a sense of connection to another."[5] Research has shown that self-disclosure fostered by a compassionate presence of another increases social bonds, which in turn reduces individual stress as well as encourages others to do the same, which can take root in a society to reduce more widespread social tension.[6] Our schools are the breeding ground for social formations, fostering or inhibiting the abilities to empathize and develop self-efficacy which leads to positive emotion and self-fulfillment; these attributes are anything but selfish. They are necessary components to the holistic approach to educational reform at its best.

Alice Isen, along with her colleagues at Cornell University, has conducted many of the key studies on the effects of happiness on thinking, and twenty years of experiments have confirmed that when people feel good, their thinking becomes more creative, integrative, flexible and open to information.

What does this have to do with education? Our schools house the young and fertile intellects of students, the minds that are wired for plasticity of growth, learning and change. What we experience in life literally changes and shapes the physical structure of the brain. It is within the context of school, the opportunities for social connectedness, that children and adolescents become aware of whom they are through the eyes of one another, looking outside themselves for approval and affirmation.

Our children and adolescents arrive in our classrooms for 10-40 or more hours a week. It is the *privilege* of educators to explore compassion and the deep reserves of our common humanity as we engage with one another. We begin this process when we forge relationships with our students, administrators, colleagues and parents. This is classroom management in its finest moment. To learn and explore happiness in relation to academic relevancy and meaning is not a luxury or by product of bonding with a student. It is a necessity. In his book *The Ultimate Happiness Prescription*, Deepak Chopra states, "An old way of being happy has brought the world to the brink of peril. A new way of being happy can save it. All the problems we see around us are the result of individuals making choices."[7]

Chopra explains, "The roots of unhappiness are often invisible. This is especially true of the conditioning that creates toxicity in a person's life. It begins in the first year of a child's life, as the infant brain learns how to think, feel, and behave from influences in the home. Conditioning becomes a dominant feature in all of us by the time we're toddlers. This is when we set lifelong patterns into our brains. Even today you are replaying scenarios you learned when you were two or three."[8]

When persons look to life and happiness without questioning their beliefs or exploring their thoughts and feelings, they tend to repeat the same circumstances and experiences over and over, feeling a familiar disappointment. Again, why do I bring this up in the context of teaching and learning? It is crucial that we teach and model shifts in perspective, because we now know our brains are wired for novel and creative learning. Cellular structures and neural connections change with experience. As educators, we have been given the opportunity to create enhanced environments and cultures that can be inspiring, novel and complex; all states of mind that engineer the mind to create and learn.

When we are able to envision the best in anyone or any situation, this process of creative visualization literally and directly affects the chemical and electrical composition of our cellular health, and that of the person we are assisting. "We have a global stake in creating happiness that is true and enduring,"[9] explains Deepak Chopra. I believe that self-awareness, while discovering one positive aspect of another, leads to healing the wounds of global unrest. Our students are reaching out to us for something, anything that feels better than what is. I believe when we are able to shift to a brighter perspective, seeing a new landscape, our children and young adults will follow.

When asked how to prevent wars of all kinds, J Krishnamurti replied, "Change yourself. Your own anger and violence are the cause of all wars." [10] I believe one of the most lethal wars leading to all wars is one with ourselves. These wars require a weapon of mass destruction—a heartfelt and ever-changing perspective.

Fall 1988
Mohawk Trails Elementary

The tension and malicious words struck the late afternoon classroom with the unexpected and brutal force of an ambush. Running through the door, Brad screamed language I was not prepared to handle. Three years prior, these words were not a part of my training as I arrogantly or maybe innocently sat in room 124 of Jordan Hall studying the pragmatic strategies and techniques of behavior management and Individualized Education Plans in one of many special education courses.

As he slammed his books on the desk and flung his chair against the wall, the class was startled into a quiet that I dreaded… Noise. I pleaded for any noise because it was much easier to swallow my ego and pride when there was classroom chaos distracting and drowning out my ineffectiveness as a young teacher as the vulgar words poised in midair ,leaving me feeling helpless and alone. I just stood there frozen for 10 or 15 seconds, waiting for a bigger, more experienced person… just anyone to step in and make this all go away. It didn't happen. I felt the sweat forming above my eyes and pooling under my arms. A distant pounding of a heart beating at an uncomfortable pace somewhere announced its cadence in my ears. Hearing Brad's rapid breathing as his head slumped forward, seeming to hang by a thread with all he had left, I hesitantly approached his desk. "I'm so sorry, Brad. I am so sorry." That is all I could say.

Maybe it would be enough?

December 2010

Twenty-one years later, recalling that afternoon and still feeling its contentious effects, I know and understand those words, "I am sorry," were enough. They were enough because some place deep down beyond textbooks, courses, and intense teacher training, my heart took over and responded from a place of understanding that couldn't be taught. Brad did not give up in school, and though he had difficult days, as his home environment continued to present stressful and oppressed experiences, he discovered the steadfast reserves in his heart that innately belonged to him.

Three weeks ago I received a call from Brad, now 32 years old. He asked if we could meet for coffee. I was overwhelmed with the thought of reconnecting with him once again. As I shuffled, stalling, and shuffling some more across Guilford Avenue, I hesitantly walked through the double glass doors of the small coffee shop in Broadripple, my head filled with questions as to how this meeting would unfold. My shuffling and doubts disappeared as his familiar grin greeted me at the corner two top. The small gas flames burning inside the circular stone fireplace reflected the warmth felt in my chest as a young man timidly waved his arm in the air, calling me back… back into that classroom of learning and teaching so many years ago. We talked about life and the places we had traveled. Preparing to leave, I began digging for my keys from the bottom of my purse. It was somewhere in that moment a mountain of gratitude leaped inside every cell of my body—for Brad had found a place in the world and was living well.

Brad taught me much that afternoon in 1988, as I found the eyes to see and an eager response from my heart, affecting a constructive difference in both our lives.

Making Contact

I believe
The greatest gift
I can conceive of having

from anyone
Is
To be seen by them,
To be understood
And
touched by them.
The greatest gift
I can give
Is
To see, hear and understand
And to touch
another person.
When this is done
I feel
contact has been made.

~ Virginia Satir

Challenges or Problems

All of these questions lead to an overall challenge or problem within our educational system and in our lives. The problem is that we are trying to save another, spinning in cycles of quick fixes and short-term solutions, looking outside ourselves, not understanding that the only person or persons to be saved and understood are ourselves. Now, to break down this challenge further, think about the day-to-day scenarios within the school environment. We hire new administrators, create magnet and charter schools, and inculcate new legislation with revamped academic standards, evaluations and progress reports. We hire curriculum specialists and create entrepreneur leaders for innovative new leadership programs, while infiltrating transition-to-teaching programs into failing schools.

We experience educational growth, no doubt. But is it lasting? Are students engaged? Will they take the content learned and lessons memorized into their daily lives, applying these concepts to tacit aptitudes in other areas as they relate to people and develop self-management proficiency, alongside terminal feelings of self-worth?

So what is the solution? The solution begins with in-depth discussions and a vigorous look inside our own values, intentions, and goals. Children and adolescents innately intuit when adults in their world are experiencing stress and negative emotions. When we are open to our own dilemmas and unmet needs, we become authentic and powerful role models for our children and students. When we share our visions and dreams, children mimic and are inspired by our presence and our shared thoughts and feelings. Children are experts at picking up on the discrepancies of who we are and who we say we are.

Exploring relational learning and creating emotional connections are part of the teaching process. We begin to explore the "process" of inquiry, service, story-telling and perspective as the challenges and solutions are explored through this book. Maybe we have become so conditioned to respond to solutions and answers that the "process" is never seen as an end, a way to improve and enhance a system that is starving for unity and simple understanding.

Chris Prentiss, author of several books on personal growth and co-founder and director of Passages Addiction Cure Center, says that to achieve personal and lasting happiness, one must be happy. That's it. It's just that simple. How can this be? When students are unhappy and teachers and administrators are frustrated and filled with angst, learning simply does not occur. Why? This notion of frustration is wrapped in a bounded and narrowed perspective. We lose the opportunity to open to awareness reflecting a depth of understanding when we hold onto anger or any negative emotion for too long. The frustration and anger can be productive in highlighting contrast, but only for a brief period. Then it is time to change our thoughts about the person or situation that stirred the unrest inside us. When we choose to see and tell a "new story," those around us cannot help but feel encouraged and participate.

What does it look like when we teach from the heart? As parents, educators, and administrators, we desire to know. We desire to know because in almost every educational or parenting self-help book or journal, there is a constant stream of thought whispering, *Come from the heart.* How does this look and feel in our classrooms and homes? It begins to feel calmer when we stop in the moment of a heated conflict and ask a five or six word question: *What can I do to help? What do you need? How may I serve you?*

Then we listen. We allow some silence as we move to the place where words are no longer needed. I have discovered that it is **never** someone or something outside myself that is the irritant or cause of the building frustration, but the negative emotion seems to result from the thoughts I hold about that situation or person. When we play these negative thoughts over and over in our minds, they become stuck, rigid and constricted. This previous statement is difficult for most people to hear, as we have been conditioned to believe that we are victims in our lives with little control or opportunity to shift how we feel. When we take a few minutes to breathe in and out, monitoring such discord, becoming aware of a grander landscape, we then can reassess.

We return to the individual or event, asking the question that boosts everyone's well-being: *How may I serve you?* What can I do to help? Please let me know what you need. Moreover, these questions generate a depth of understanding we lacked in the beginning. When we examine and explore every conflict and disagreement, whether in schools or in our homes, we will discover that seated at the root of most divisive thoughts are misunderstandings and perspectives that have narrowed with the onset of anger and frustration. But we have the freedom to choose how we respond every time there is an exchange of words and feelings inside any disagreeable or ornery encounter. We now know that the brain is capable and wired to freely choose thoughts that either feel fearful, neutral or joyful. When the brain registers feelings of safety and security, teachers are given the green light to pique interests, ignite the imagination, and fuel the fires of creative learning. This is when and where we raise test scores, but more importantly, observe a child engaged in the process of learning, excited about the possibilities.

Pleasure transforms a world, not coercion.

~ Ralph Waldo Emerson

A few years ago, someone exasperated with my questions and dialogues said, "Lori, the only life you can save is your own." At first I thought this statement sounded selfish and unrealistic, almost paradoxical to the premise of this story; but as I pondered the statement, it began to feel more accurate and applicable. I felt it was true for my students as well. *How may I serve you?* The question assists us in moving within, toward the intelligence of the heart, where our intuitive responses are explored.

Intuition

Intuition is the power of knowing things without conscious reasoning, and this is where we begin to serve another. We listen within, where our hearts understand and respond with clarity, reaching beneath behaviors, words and actions. We need to encourage one another to trust that inner voice, that inner teacher who knows and recognizes well-being. *When I am experiencing happiness and feeling secure in who I am, there is much of myself to share with others.* A slice of my joy and contentment becomes another's joy and contentment. They are truly physiologically, psychologically and socially contagious, these feelings of well-being when we choose to serve from the heart.

The statement, "The only life you can save is your own," echoes in my mind as I walk into classrooms and down the halls of schools in the inner city of Indianapolis. When we spend time worrying and obsessing over seemingly negative situations we encounter, we are unable to open to a perspective that benefits and shifts a situation into a powerful learning episode. How different the outcome would be if we trusted that our co-workers, partners, parents, and students have all they need to learn and grow in a world that often feels troubled and fragile. I once read that as a culture, we do not take pleasure seriously enough. I feel this to be true in education. The joy of learning has lost its way into many of our hearts and classrooms, but I am hopeful these joys will return —one student, one teacher and one school at a time.

Education: Past Present and Future

Our brains are wired for many purposes, but survival, novelty, emotional expression and questions enter into this discussion. Eric Jenson reports that "the brain is more receptive to questions about new knowledge than to answers because curiosity is a distinct physiological state that triggers changes in our posture and eye movements, promoting chemical reactions that are advantageous to learning and recall."[11] I find it interesting that the brain continues to process questions long after they have been asked and sometimes answered.

How is this brain information aligned with our current educational directives and core standard and assessment emphasis? Research has also determined that the brain thrives on meaningful and relevant information stimulated by emotions and an academic curriculum that pulls from a student's personal and prior life experiences. Obviously, we are unable to create and present relevant and meaningful content one hundred percent of the time, but we can hold awareness for the importance of these brain and emotion driven teaching and learning strategies as we begin to design content that drives student excitement and mastery.

The relationships we develop in and out of school cannot help but affect the acquisition and retention of new knowledge. Michael Anderson, a third-year teacher in Indianapolis, Indiana, and cohort member of the Indianapolis Teaching Fellows, a national teaching transition program, was recently selected as teacher of the year for the Indianapolis Public Schools. He says his recipe for success in the classroom is simple: "Earn students' respect, create an environment where it's safe for them to try and fail, and then make the material relevant to their lives." Anderson believes the first step in becoming and being a strong educator is to build an emotional connection with students. Some of his students won't even try to work in other classes but will pour amazing amounts of energy into his class, Michael reports.

We are social beings, learning through the experiences of one another in how we communicate and express feelings and thoughts. When we are told there is one way, or one response, a natural inbred resistance surfaces. In his book *The Element*, Ken Robinson stresses contrast of conformity and creativity in schools and the historical implications:

> Public education puts relentless pressure on its students to conform. Public schools were not only created in the interests of industrialism—they were created in the image of industrialism. They reflect the factory culture they were designed to support. Secondary education mimics this concept with the construction of an assembly line mentality and the division of labor. Schools divide the curriculum into segments, arranging the days into blocks of time as students are educated in batches according to age and given standardized tests as

> set points compared with each other before going
> out into the market place.12

For those students who work well from a structured, linear, math and language format, this type of system has been beneficial and successful, but it is not for everyone. When we take an in-depth look at the intimate relationship between learning, emotional connections and the totality of brain function, we recognize the unintentional limits we have placed on the proliferation of imaginative and critical thinking, even from those students who seem to fare well from the more traditional school instruction and setting.

The Element

The experiences and beliefs we hold in life initiate an array of feelings and cognitive implications: apathy, excitement, passion, hopelessness, innovation, expressive learning, and profound retention. When we pay attention to how we feel, we are guided into what Ken Robinson, author and educator, calls our *element*. He states, "Finding your *element* is essential to your well-being, ultimate success, and to the health of our organizations and effectiveness of our educational system... One's *element* is the meeting point between natural aptitude and personal passion." 13 Our children are born with an excitement to explore, ask questions, and imagine that anything and everything is possible. We were born with a mind that is wired to create and expand, embracing novelty and curiosity.

Daniel Pink discusses a movement in education and business that he describes as "High Concept and High Touch." According to Pink, *high concept* involves "the ability to create artistic and emotional beauty, to detect patterns and opportunities, to craft a satisfying narrative and to combine seemingly unrelated ideas into novel innovations." 14 *High touch* is "the ability to empathize, to understand the inner workings and importance of relational learning, discovering deeper meaning and purpose while finding joy in one's self, therefore eliciting it in others." 15 These notions will drive deeper learning in schools and in education as a whole.

They also carry the potential to tap into the passions of students who have been unintentionally academically neglected in a world dominated by left-brain-directed teaching. Both hemispheres of the brain are needed to live in this world, but as a society, we have not recognized the importance of the right brain's functions as we move into a new *conceptual era* where *high concept and high touch learning and interacting* will be the new societal norm. The right brain allows us to see whole pictures, synthesizing information, using the seemingly unrelated parts to create a solution or design that we didn't notice when looking at the details and parts of a presented challenge or problem. The right hemispheric brain allows us to comprehend metaphors, understanding how something is stated or expressed, recognizing the emotions that accompany the words. It is tempting to talk of right and left brain, but as Daniel Pink discusses, "the left and right hemispheres in isolation are actually two half-brains, designed to work together as a smooth, single, integrated whole in one complete brain." 16

There are thousands of brilliant educators that are and will pave the path, inspiring and motivating learners to know who they are and how they learn. These educational leaders are assisting students in discovering their passions and how to meaningfully and successfully integrate those into an academic curriculum.

The joining between educators, students and subject matter is missing inside many schools in this time. In the words of Ken Robinson, author and teacher:

The dominant Western world-view is not based on seeing synergies and connections, but on making distinctions and seeing differences. Much of Western thought assumes that the mind is separate from the body and that human beings are somehow separate from the rest of nature. Maybe this is why so many people don't seem to understand that what we put into our bodies affects how it works and how we think and feel.[17]

Holistic education has the capability of bridging the gaps of body, mind and spirit. It is a process of reaching within, exploring thoughts, feelings, and what we emotionally and physically ingest. Holistic education gives meaning and understanding to how we interact inside a world that was designed for introspective awareness, connections, and relationships. We sit beside one another and design ways to encourage self-expression, increasing one's capacity for opportunities and feelings of success. We do this beginning with the smallest of steps and goals.

When we teach to integrate and build upon a student's strengths, it is imperative we look to the diversity in our classrooms and schools as a rich resource rather than as a problem to solve. In the book *Rethinking Disability*, Jan Valle and David Connor explain this fresh way of embracing diversity and the needs of all students: "Inclusion means that we help all children to learn and participate in meaningful ways. Thus the inclusive classroom, one driven with heart and service to another, is a nurturing learning community where everyone belongs and everyone benefits."[18]

Humans are the only species that intuit the awareness of **how** we perceive, feel and interact inside a world where self-inflicted illness and suicide rates are soaring. Statistics report that hundreds of millions of people are moving through their days relying on prescription drugs to treat emotional disorders. The abuse of non-prescription drugs and alcohol has skyrocketed. Ken Robinson reports from his book, *The Element*, "Death each year from suicides around the world is greater than those from armed conflicts. According to the World Health Organization, suicide is now the third highest cause of death among people aged 12 to 30." [19]

Mr. Pickett
You've Got Mail

One late Monday afternoon, while leaning over the computer frantically preparing for my Monday night class, "You've got mail" rang in my ears. Looking at the address and then the subject line, my heart began that fluttering nervous beating, and a feeling of impending dread filled my body in a matter of seconds... Hesitantly I took a deep breath, then clicked the button on the mouse and began to read. "Andrew is sitting with his group and working tremendously hard on his project. He is attentive and motivated. Please let me know how I may serve you in the days and weeks to come."

Now I understood the subject line: "Andrew in action," which had brought such dread moments earlier. Those few words placed not only a smile on my face, but gave me hope that is absolutely indescribable as a mom. This teacher had taken three minutes to share his story of a teaching experience that for many would have gone unnoticed. Mr. Pickett was able to embrace another perspective, seeing the heart in this young man who had been recently struggling in a world of adolescent chaos. When I read the e-mail to Andrew a few hours later, he beamed with renewed confidence, and his effort and grades in this class soared during the remainder of the semester. I will never forget this experience as an educator, but mostly as a mom. I watched the gradual and extraordinary shift in Andrew's self-confidence that a few sincere words created in his life and in mine.

Remember and Begin

I was once told that if you ask the questions, sitting quietly in their mystery, not needing or seeking solutions or answers, you will spin an acceptance of the question and quite possibly discover solutions or alternate responses you never imagined... I'm beginning to grasp this notion somewhat playfully, as are many of my teachers and students.

Is life to be creative and pleasurable, or are we to feel increased suffering and a stifling gloom of circumstances as we mature and leave our childhoods? I never truly understood how so many children living carefree in one moment evolve into adolescents and adults who seemed to land, then continuously float in pools of self-perceived stress and hopelessness. Do we not create cycles of victimhood by our worn-out, repetitive thoughts and behaviors? I understand that with the progression of age comes financial responsibility, job security, and the complexities of family life. But where did we lose this sense of curiosity, creativity and awe for just breathing in and out?

What do any of these aforementioned statements and questions have to do with *revelations in education*? They have *everything* to do with education. Our ways of being in the world often begin in our classrooms. Many of our initial social experiences and formal knowledge introductions occurred in schools alongside teachers. How did this feel? What are our memories of these first experiences when peers, desks, rules and books dominated our days, leaving us bereft of playing and make-believing?

As a mother, teacher, and student participating in public schools for many years, I wonder about the atrophied young minds of many of our students, where imagination and creativity are buried. When did this happen, and how do we assist our students in uncovering the magic of a question asked and a problem explored? Have our notions and ideals about education contributed to the complacency and slow-to-change ideology in our schools across the nation and world? Do higher test scores, longer school days, and an emphasis on math, technology, and science seal the deal for successful and happy students and educators? Definitively, no. Look around, read, observe and listen to conversations surrounding education.

Exploring and redefining the role of teachers and education is worthy of discussion as the environment and therefore the brains of our students have changed. Experiences in life shape our brains; the actual physiological structure changes when we are exposed to novelty or unfamiliar events.

Because we are living in a fast-paced and technologically advanced culture and complex age of information, technology changes every couple of months. Many of the careers and occupations our students will be employed in are not even known as I write these words. It is imperative we engage passion, intuition and creativity in developing independent thinkers in today's educational world. Innovation, imagination and inquiry will be incentives and an inherent part in a world of global markets, operative organizations and extraordinary careers not yet known.

Stress

There have been research studies conducted on the heightened stress levels of adolescents who text from their cell phones hundreds of times every day. Eric Jenson reports that the prevalence of children with a chronic or acute stress disorder is 18-20%.[20] The largest group of stress-disordered individuals is school-age children. Jenson explains, "Stress is a physiological response to a perspective. The perspective originates from a feeling of lack of control over a situation or environment. When this state occurs, a hyper secretion of cortisol, a stress related hormone, takes place when the body experiences stress." [21] It is known among neuroscientists and now educators that the memory and mental clarity required in learning new concepts is greatly affected and declines when stress is present and activated in a child or adolescent's body.

Although the math and science scores are lower in the United States than in many Asian countries, a recent international study reported the following:

Chinese children as young as six are suffering from serious stress at school, according to the international study, which shines a light onto the pressures faced by Chinese youngsters being pushed to take advantage of the opportunities of the "new" China. A scientific survey of 9 to 12-year-olds in eastern China found that more than 80 percent worried "a lot" about exams, two-thirds feared punishment by their teachers, and almost three-quarters reported fearing physical punishment from their parents.22

There is always a tradeoff and balancing mechanism in place when we consciously or subconsciously move to one extreme or the other in any area of life. When we push our children and students to strive academically, neglecting emotional intelligence and social connectedness, there are often times negative consequences within the social and emotional constructs of development. If we do not set high expectations and place pertinent and meaningful content while differentiating instruction into our curriculum, we may see apathetic students who do not embrace the importance and significance of learning and inquiry.

Whether we like it or not, agree or disagree, this is a technologically accelerated and communicative culture in which children and adolescents are spending more alone time with technology and less time in familial circles, where affirmation and support from extended family and friends have resided in years past. Could our classrooms provide a place of support, embracing a safe and nurturing sea of acceptance where feelings of security and empathetic listening are grounded in daily procedures? Here is the place where diversity of student population is celebrated. I believe that many classrooms are already fostering enriched environments, but there is more…

Could a compassionate presence in education be the cornerstone for bringing meaning and relevancy to a holistic platform of simply living life? I believe the answer is yes.

When children and adolescents are attending school 40 or more hours a week, we need to address and be respectful of the social, emotional and cognitive implications. Could education in our schools across the world become the basis for teaching and generating compassion? As educators serving all ages and grades, we carry the capacity for assisting our students with compassionate learning through exploring awareness and purposes in education and in life. We will further discuss these notions.

Questions are fueled by curiosity and a desire to understand the matrices of human relationships, emotions, and *how* people think. Education is the hub in the wheel of life, and although this statement may feel simplistic or tired, it's possible that *we teach what we need to learn*. So it is with this desire to *question* and to understand the intimate entanglement of life and its relationships: that education is the engine of this story, one written and read by all of us.

My excitement is genuine and hard to contain when I think of our children and the meeting of minds where teacher and student begin deeply listening to one another. I ask and sometimes plead with my graduate students to listen to their hearts, discovering the meaning and purpose beneath the surface of every behavior. I must model this request in my own life, a process which is not so easy and one that takes time. Listen to your heart—don't settle for "what is."

Thoughts, Perspectives, and Teachers

Research has reported that it is rarely the event or experience that causes distress in our lives. It is usually the interaction between the event and our learned coping skills. Our coping skills are constructed and supported by our social and familial conditioning, belief systems, and the thoughts we exercise day to day.

In many facets of life, we sometimes consciously or subconsciously limit our creative potential. We do this through our thinking. We limit many of the possibilities and dreams we imagined in an earlier time, abandoning them for something easier, more accessible, or more convenient. We limit our thinking by our repetitive thoughts and habitual behaviors, and then adamantly complain about our lives and those around us. Why?

As teachers, we have forgotten that our greatest teachers are our students. If we are to make a difference in the lives of our learners, positing the changes we desire, isn't it time to awaken to this perspective? How do we discover a hidden jewel beneath a sarcastic comment or a glimmer of passion inside an adolescent temper tantrum or disruptive behavior? I'm not suggesting we ignore the inappropriateness of students' behaviors and acts of insubordination, but I do believe we never solve an issue by punishing without understanding the origin of actions and words. Positive classroom engagement must incorporate facets of deep understanding and reflection so we are preventing repetitive cycles of unproductive and inappropriate behaviors. Treating the symptoms and band-aiding the reoccurring scab without examining the infection zaps our energy and keeps teacher, student and parent battling with the non-issue, the dysfunctional surface. Let us listen and move to empathic understanding, where the source of relationships is waiting for exploration.

Imagination and School?

When did we stop imagining? When did we become participants in life who settle for what is, hoping for something better to come along? What is happening within our society when the headlines scream of homicides, gang activities, suicides, brokenness, and human suffering? Even bullying has taken on another dimension in cyberspace. Where is the good news, and what does it have to do with *education revelation? Classrooms are the launching pads for formal training in academic acquisition, but more importantly, for developing relationships and acquiring life skills for a compassionate living curriculum.* Abraham Lincoln said, "Upon the subject of education, I view it as the most important subject who we as a people can be engaged in." Research has shown that next to a parent, a teacher is the most significant adult in a child's life.

When children enter a classroom for the first time at five years of age, typically their spirits are not broken, nor do they spend endless hours sitting in negative emotion. But if their spirits feel broken and they have experienced challenging events in their young lives, as teachers, we must be prepared to **serve** all their needs, prioritizing and understanding the whole child. Children are not born hating or filled with rage for those persons who are *perceived* to be so radically different. Have you ever walked by an unknown three-, four- or five-year-old and he shouts out, "Hi!" without hesitation. I smile just writing these words, because children's young minds are accepting, not seeing color, size, or differences that create defensive responses adults generate.

Five- and six-year-olds ask great questions and explore what is around them, declaring what is good and feels right. How did we lose this sense of wonder, confidence, and awe as we progressed from grade to grade?

The Heart of the Matter

How can we embrace life, *an extended compassionate education* led by the heart? Maybe we begin by recognizing that the force and electromagnetic field of the heart is more powerful than the brain. The heart has an intelligence of its own, with forty to sixty times the electrical amplitude of the brain, as reported by the HeartMath Institute.[23] Researchers have found that positive emotions not only increase coherent heart rhythms, but enhance cognitive functioning and mental clarity.[24] When teachers and students are experiencing less stress and anxiety in the classroom, the level of compatibility, compassion and positive emotion directly contributes to improved social, emotional and academic performance. Inside the heart is where goose bumps and tears take formation as feelings drive our intentions to dream, imagine, learn and remember. The heart teaches us about perspective and the powerful guidance of our emotions, breeding an intelligence of its own, when we gear up, open up and listen.

We begin to ask the essential questions when we come from the place of the heart—*How may I serve you?* What will it take to highlight and place the successful stories of teacher/student partnerships on the front pages of newspapers and major newscasts? We collectively understand the domino effect and the intense following of news stories generated by drama and fear. Isn't it time for a collective broadcast ignited by stories demonstrating compassion and service for one another?

Over a year ago I watched a professional athlete apologize for personal choices he had made in his past. This confession or explanation was being broadcast over every major television channel, followed by discussions and perspectives of many, who in reality have no idea what rests in the heart of another. Isn't it time to shift our priorities, generating a leading edge interest in educational triumphs interrupting regularly scheduled broadcasts where teachers, parents and students discover compassionate learning with the potential to change a world? I'm ready for the good news, delving into stories about the rekindled imaginations of students in classrooms and those teachers who have filled their students' minds with strength of purpose. I am excited to read and retell the stories about the literacy improvements, but more important in the twenty-first century are the creative and imaginative improvements through a teaching heart for thousands of children in urban schools. I am eager to read and share stories about groups of children who made a discovery on the playground and are tracking their findings through a homemade device created by their classmates. These stories must continually ring out on World News Tonight. When our minds are filled with visions of possibility, we begin to experience the miracles of innovation and passionate learning. The positive emotions that inspiration and possibility create are contagious. We become a people of hope, and our children learn this quickly if they are **not** pointed in the direction of lack and fear.

Compassionate Presence—National Core Standard

"Compassion" derives from the Latin *patior* and the Greek *pathein*, "to suffer, undergo or experience." It means "to endure [something] with another person." Compassion is a virtue which requires us to put ourselves consistently in another's shoes, to feel his or her pain as though it were our own, and to enter generously into her point of view. This is summed up in the Golden Rule: "Do not do to others what you would not like them to do to you," or, in its positive form, "Always treat others as you wish to be treated yourself." You have to look into your own heart, *discover what gives you pain, and then refuse—under any circumstance whatsoever—to inflict that pain on anybody else.*

After reviewing a few different definitions of compassion, my understanding is that to have compassion means that you actually feel the suffering of another, and this inspires the desire and the will to make a positive action on the other's behalf. If we are truly to inspire compassion in the minds and hearts of our student population, then we will need to actively create a national compassionate standard. The standard should address the emotional, social and relational components, bringing to light a holistic education. This curriculum will need to intimately tie emotions and learning into a matrix of brain-based teaching and learning. In the epilogue, I have created a core outline for a national standard of compassionate teaching and learning. This outline discusses the goals, activities, materials and projects teachers, students, parents and the community at large would endorse and place into action. At some point, I hope I have an opportunity to be an active participant in working toward such a significant aspect of educational reform.

The following study by Dr. Caron Goode revealed: "Compassion is the desire to assuage feelings of suffering in others. A compassionate person considers the sufferings of others as his own. But compassion is not pity and it is also different from altruism, which is simply an action of helping others. Compassion is a combination of feeling for someone else, experiencing the suffering and a positive move to reduce the suffering of others."

Today there is a need to make specific efforts to teach compassion to children for several reasons:

• Competitive environments force us to be cut-throat— High levels of competition in society are not limited to only the workplace, but have percolated down to academics and children's sports. Even young toddlers are not spared by this bogeyman of vying for the best position in class or the maximum attention of the teacher.

• Violence in the media and environment—Our children today are more exposed to violence due to television programs and video games that in turn tend to increase violence in children themselves. A review done by NCTV in 1990 found that 75% of the studies that were done on the effect of video games on normal children reported that video games had harmful effects. Psychologists Craig A. Anderson, Ph. D., and Karen E. Dill, Ph. D., have said, "the study reveals that even a brief exposure to violent video games can temporarily increase aggressive behavior in all types of participants."[1] 25

Teaching compassion can create awareness in the minds of our students and the world around them. When compassion is ignited, children and adolescents learn to be more sensitive and caring towards one another, but the skill of "empathy" is actively implemented.

Dr. Dan Siegel, author, motivational speaker and psychiatrist, explains an important relational skill inherent in all people called *emotional contagion*. Persons seem to automatically sense an internal state of mind of another person. This inter-connectedness is based on the neurological connections from mirror neurons that are activated and mirrored when we experience actions or words from one another. When I watch a movie that is sad, I cry even though this is not a part of my personal experience. We yawn when we observe yawning in another. These examples are the results of activated mirror neurons. In his most recent book, entitled *Mindsight*, Dan Seigel explains,

> The internal states of others—from joy and play to sadness and fear—directly affect our own state of mind. This contagion can even make us interpret unrelated events with an uncertain bias—so for example, after we've been around someone who is depressed, we interpret someone else's seriousness as sadness.... Our awareness of another person's state of mind depends on how well we know our own—we notice the belly fill with laughter at a party or with sadness at the funeral home. This is the main reason that people who are more aware of their bodies have been found to be more empathetic." 26

In conclusion, when we are aware and open to our own feelings and emotions, the primary pathway for how well we resonate with others and sense their state of mind and accompanying feelings is wide open.

I once read that the vital difference between a good teacher and one that is superior is the teacher who self-reflects. After reading the notions and research of Dr. Siegel, I feel this statement could lead to compelling positive changes in *how* we relate and therefore reach out to all students, but especially those who dare us to teach them. Do we reflect and think about how we perceive the world? Do we transfer our own emotions subconsciously or consciously onto those who walk into our classrooms each day? I think these questions are worth thinking about as we examine and explore compassionate instruction inside our schools.

What Do You Need?

When will the state superintendent come to the second grade teacher and ask, "How may I serve you?" When will the Title One seventh grade teacher come to the parents and ask, "What do you need?" When will the students sent to detention return to their teacher and state, "We're sorry, can we begin again?" When will the parents reach out to the teacher with heartfelt thanks for her expressed compassion in the classroom? When will the administration come to its faculty with one intention: "How can I help in creating a happier and more productive semester for you? What do you need?"

In my own life, when I ask my students, family or friends, *What can I do? How can I help you?* or *What do you need?* I must listen deeply. When I listen, I'm able to observe... then understand the meaning of a response beyond the uttered words or platitudes of presence. Forfeiting deep listening, I fall back to the ways of correction, rapidly searching for solutions and quick fixes. It is difficult to listen and then rest with the discomfort of not knowing. Sharing this discomfort with our students seeds an authentic trust and mutual respect.

When will teacher and student see one another in the mirror of possibilities, where many of the answers to life's questions are found in the eyes of our perceived adversaries? There are times when persons feel a connectedness to another though they may not discuss or explore its meaning. How often have we felt disgruntled, annoyed, or in contrast, just peaceful in the presence of a relative, friend, colleague, student or even stranger? *The energy of those around us delivers awareness about ourselves IF we are open to discovery.*

Projection can be defined as subconsciously allocating to another those feelings and thoughts that plague or interfere with our perception of an experience or situation. Every person projects his thoughts and feelings at one time, and it is with awareness when we do that we benefit from the occurrence. Teachers and students spend several hours a week communicating, verbally and nonverbally, *how each is connecting to the other.* Self-awareness of this interaction is an inherent part of effective communication and behavior engagement in any classroom. Power struggles and irritations between teachers and students often escalate when one is unaware and reacting to a chain of perceived misgivings. These negative emotions create narrowed thinking when we are confronted with solving a problem or discovering a solution. Are our greatest teachers those with whom we struggle? I believe they are when hearts and eyes are open to this judicious perspective.

Time and Tradition

Time is moving so fast we can barely peel off the paper dates from the calendar or observe the electronic flash of a date on the screen of computers or phones before another week or month has arrived. Even children notice and comment on the rapidity of time. Driving my daughter and her friends to school each morning, the conversation inadvertently moves to "How can it be Friday again?"

It is a time of swift transition in the world and in education. Could there be an evolving death of traditional instructional strategies, managing classrooms, and training teachers, giving birth to an emotional and social educational intelligence? There is much dissension and discussion emerging from the educational vista, and this is good because chaos and change produce results.

Jimmy is 12 years old and lives inside an autistic world. Sitting in the third row of his general education math class, he has 18 minutes, give or take a few, until the bell rings dismissing the students for the day. He feels the powerful urge to go the bathroom and waves his hand in the air, desperately at-

tempting to get the teacher's full attention. When she finally turns around and acknowledges Jimmy's flailing arms, he loudly proclaims that he must be excused right now. "Jimmy, you will need to wait a few more minutes as we are in the middle of the lesson, and unless this is an emergency, please wait." Jimmy has been taught the definition of an emergency, and from his literal perspective, this urge to go to the bathroom doesn't qualify. He asks again a bit more loudly. The teacher ignores the question, and frustrated beyond class rules, Jimmy stands up and shouts, "You are nothing but a mediocre trumpet player!" He proceeds to march out of the room. This may not mean much to you if you are not familiar with Spongebob Squarepants, *a popular cartoon on television, but this comment did get the teacher's attention, and Jimmy incurred negative consequences and admonishment from his teacher and much laughter from his friends for his truthful response.*

It is from this story that the wisdom, heart and understanding we attempt to embrace for each of our students is **service and teaching** at its finest. We are not the controllers and experts in our classrooms. When we begin to understand this imperative perspective, we embark on a journey where we learn more than we teach, and therefore our instruction and understanding of the educational process improves and affects positive changes.

In years past, many educators and parents have isolated ourselves inside the Trojan horse of content expertise and child development, where we have been conditioned to believe that students desperately need our cognitive and behavioral fixes and solutions. Could this singular thinking and outdated attitude embracing control and power monopolize the thought processes of those within the political arenas and upper echelons of public instruction and higher education?

They were seated around long conference tables in padded chairs that spin. Presidents, governors, state superintendents, superintendents, administrators, and CEO's of large companies desirous of opening charter schools and expanding their institutions with policy reforms, consciously or subconsciously placing themselves in positions of superiority. When carrying an agenda of perceived expertise, persons in leadership capacities can unwillingly and un-knowingly create opposition and quiet dissension without words being spoken.

"How may I serve you?" a young man gently inquires during an intense gathering of board members discussing data retrieval and annual yearly progress presented from inner city charter schools. Heads turn and all are silent. The young board member, a new first-year teacher invited to the meeting, subtly smiles and pulls from his backpack a handwritten proposal on a pad of yellow legal paper. With a pen in his hand and sleeves rolled up, his eyes skim the perplexed looks on the faces around the table. Smiling, he repeats the question...

Projects

Last semester in our concluding graduate class, I asked the teachers/students to present their final projects sharing their blue prints of an inclusive classroom, a classroom that was the ultimate expression in emotional, physical, and collaborative effect promoting heightened interest, passionate learning and a heart for life skills. The students were informed that the project could be presented in the format and style that best suited their learning style and personal strengths. Jeff Truelock, a first-year secondary math teacher and graduate student with the Indianapolis Teaching Fellows, wrote an outstanding proposal to the President of the United States. What follows is an excerpt of Jeff's letter and brilliantly written proposal emphasizing the importance of relationship and brain-based education inside our classrooms.

Abstract

This proposal to the United States Federal Government is a brief request to initiate a nationwide assault on education. The author believes that the deconstructing of methods of old and the rebuilding of a timely and more globally relevant education system is overdue and imperative to the success and security of the United States. The author makes claims which are supported by extensive research and practicality of brain-based inclusion teaching methods and techniques.

Final Blueprint Project
Federally Funded Brain-Based Inclusive Classroom Proposal

In sharp contrast to old-school lectures and pop quizzes to scare students into learning, this project seeks to encourage the involvement of students in their own learning from the beginning to the end; from creating the test to grading it and analyzing mistakes. Students who are cognizant of what is expected of them and have the opportunity to illustrate their mastery of the standards in the style in which they feel most comfortable, instead of being cornered into one high-stakes multiple choice test, research shows that these students are more likely to succeed (Stiggins, 2008). Moreover, it is in our nature as humans to perform up to standards when we know exactly what is expected of us. Why would we deny our students the same courtesy and not include them in their own learning? The days of fear reigning in the classroom are long since passed. The days of progressive education are upon us, and as educators, if we fail to seize the methods and include our students from the very beginning, we are working in vain and our fruits will spoil over one short summer break.

As one of my heroes, educator and author Rafe Esquith, would say, "We can do better." I am a middle school math teacher; not working for the government (maximizing my degree in Russian language), because I know we can do better. Volunteering in the Campaign for Change as a block captain in Southern Indiana and seeing what can happen when we all work together continues to give me the confidence to take on the challenge of teaching in a high needs urban school; and I am reminded that we can do better. I love my students and am serving my country in a way that I never thought possible. I have dispensed with the idea of government work or attending law school, and plan to remain in the classroom for as long as my superiors allow. So, after my first year teaching, I feel bold enough, and somehow connected to the Administration, to ask for your consideration of a Federally Funded Brain-Based Inclusive Classroom Program (FBICP) to be piloted in six states in three different regions of the country for two years. The number of schools with brain-based inclusive curricula doubles every two-year term given at least a 90% increase in achievement until all public school systems in the United States thusly operate. Funds for this program can be made available by implementing hefty fines for cell phone usage on federal highways, taxing big oil, and using funds already existing in the federal education budget allocated for technology. Unions would also be encouraged to contribute to the new FBICP, as would private donors and philanthropic organizations and individuals.

As a first-year teacher, I have realized that teaching to a high stakes test is really all a teacher has time to do. Between the redundant "professional development" sessions that are required by the school district in which I work, and the mediocre classes that I am required to take in order to earn a Master's in Teaching and become certified as a middle school math teacher in Indiana, there are few days to actually teach the material that my students have to master before high stakes assessments that are given at a rate of five tests every 18 weeks. The work is not the issue. It can be done and it is being done every day in a middle school math classroom in Indianapolis, Indiana. The key to making this happen is 100% engagement, 100% of the time.

Engaging the students in conversation is the first step to building a safe, fun classroom environment underpinned by respect, empowerment, and inclusion. Simply being mindful of the students' techno-speak and abilities bridges most gaps to creating such an environment.

Most students at any level in their education know or remember the feeling: getting onto the bus on a cold December morning, the freezing vinyl seat creeping through hand-me-down corduroys, stomach in knots—partly because of the test you are getting ready to fail, and partly because you were afraid to/unable to eat this morning, palms sweating, clammy cheeks, and then the bell rings. If only you knew exactly what was going to be on this test. Instead, your instructor assigned a list of readings and tons of home-work problems for you to do, sometimes returning your work in time for you to use as a study guide, sometimes not. No one deserves to be treated that way. No one should be tormented or put under this much stress. There are multiple ways to assess whether or not we know what we know. Echoing educator Rick Stiggins, if we know how to find the answer, that is just as good as knowing the answer. Yet, there are many who hesitate to use or allow students to use calculators or claim that using calculators on a math test is cheating. I sincerely beg to differ. Expanding on this, I offer an analogy of the carpenter driving a nail into a wall. I ask students if they have ever seen a carpenter drive a nail with her fist. Of course they haven't. She uses her tool—her hammer. So if students use a graphing calculator to help them properly calculate the total of an obscene list of integers, so what! They know how to use the technology that everyone else is using in the real world to come up with answers. Moreover, technology helps improve my students' understanding vis-à-vis significant increases in their self-efficacy, respective self-images, and confidence. Undeniably, too many students are using technology everywhere but in the classroom; as they walk down the street, in the halls and bathrooms of the very schools that forbid cell phones, at home on the X-Box or Wii. There is no reason that our children should not be just as engaged in the class-room as they are when texting one another in the bath-room during fourth period.

In order to properly establish and maintain a brain-based in-clusive classroom worthy of line items in the federal education budget providing the necessary technologies to keep students en-gaged, three components must be implemented at the classroom level.

1. The classroom culture must be based in morality, from which we derive expectations, procedures and class-room guide-lines, NOT "rules." It is imperative to step out of the box of tradi-tional "rules" as this creates more power struggles between teach-er and student. I taught with a "veteran" teacher last summer and he had two separate sets of rules for his classroom: one set for the students and another for the teachers. The time I spent teaching with him during summer school was a crash course in how NOT to set up my classroom. In the FBICP classroom, guidelines are rooted in morality, as explained in Kohleberg's *Theory of Moral De-velopment*, from which stems expectations of behavior. In order for the students to understand why there are procedures for class-room activities, they must see what underlies those procedures in order to comprehend their existence. Too many of my colleagues, first- through third-year teachers, experience their greatest chal-lenges in the arena of classroom management. My colleagues' fail-ure to relate to the students on a human level, through morality, expectations, and procedures, is a significant hurdle in their ability to close the achievement gap, and I cannot help but to think that this same plaguing educator-mentality is preventing many, many more kids from seeing their full academic and social potential real-ized. The physical space of the classroom must reflect the popula-tion of the student body. That is, diversity is paramount in stu-dents' ability to reach their highest goals. Having posters repre-senting examples of masters in the subject area who reign from all countries of the earth builds and can strengthen the students' self-image and overall academic achievement. As Jaime Escalante said to motivate his students, "Math is in your blood." When the kids

realize that they are innately able to do anything, we give them technology and watch them fly.

2. Classroom management styles must be non-confrontational and respectful of students' differing and STILL DEVELOPING personality traits and temperaments. Guidelines, not rules, should be constructed as a class, teacher and students, and posted in the classroom as a reminder. If the issue of management starts with a discussion on morality with the students, the students respond positively and are engaged because they feel respected and that they are being treated as equals. Ask the students what they do face with a moral dilemma and talk it out. From this discussion comes a discussion about expectations of behavior since we are all human and will learn from one another. After expectations are discussed, the class as a whole constructs the guidelines for the classroom. The guidelines do NOT state "Students will..." Rather, the guidelines are to be inclusive of students, teachers, and anyone else who enters the classroom. The following set of guidelines is recommended:

1. We will RESPECT one another; property, spaces, and ideas.
2. We will EMPOWER one another to learn from one another.
3. We will INCLUDE one another in our reciprocal learning experiences.
4. We will ACCOUNT for one another; in and out of the classroom.

3. Powerful and meaningful experiences follow naturally when classroom management structures are in place that allow for all to feel welcome, safe, and capable of having fun. Respecting and trusting the students FIRST is imperative. For some students, this is a big first and the door is open for the manifestation of the dreams of those children. There will be those who test the system, for whom we have consequences which are fair and administered in a timely and non-embarrassing manner. Powerful and meaningful experiences can be the result of a showdown between a stu-

dent and teacher; the result of properly administered consequences. Consistency and limitations are elements that all children crave; understandably so, as they are signs of love and respect. Furthermore, when students see that they have an impact, not unlike what I saw in November of 2008, their self-efficacy can be increased and motivation is a likely result. For example, in order to teach data analysis to students, my students and I are completing a project on teen homelessness in Indianapolis. In other classes, we have learned geometry by taking the classroom outside to pick up trash and litter on campus, identifying shapes and using formulas to make calculations. When the students are able to unleash a little energy and a lot of imagination, teaching automatically becomes facilitation instead of monotonous, old-school lectures, memorization, and direct instruction.

Mr. President, I beseech you to begin true progressive education reform by initializing the FBICP. The outline of classroom level elements to be implemented has been provided in order to ensure the students' and teachers' respective abilities to be in an environment where technology and developing relationships can be continuously explored and used. All students in the pilot schools will need the following items:

- TI-84+ Texas Instruments Graphing Calculator
- iPad or PC laptop

All schools will need to be updated with the latest wireless technology and classroom technologies, such as LCD projectors and screens, document cameras, laptops/ PCs/iPads, and media towers consisting of audio/visual technologies (Blue Ray/DVD player, local cable). A specific invoice will be issued upon your approval and funding of the program.

WE can make a difference. With the proper technology and educational environments, yes we can.

Sincerely,
Jeffrey A. Truelock
Harshman Middle School, Indianapolis, Indiana

I continue to hear people speak of change occurring in the world when the year 2012 arrives. Is 2012 a literal end to the world, or an end to a world as we have known it? I believe the latter. It is my intention and desire that 2012 marks the beginning of an occasion when we explore and remember how a history of violence, hatred, and perspectives of separatism spewed us into the flames of self-righteous and fearful thinking. For when we understand this unpleasant perspective and historical condition, within any institution or system, our students will know contrast between the old and the new, therefore desiring something much different from life, relationships, and education.

Just as teachers model the steps to a math problem or discuss impressions of genres to be explored, or create an actual project that the students are expected to produce, we must always model new perspectives and alternate ways of responding to frustrating and unproductive social situations and interactions. Emotional well-being sets the stage for academic mastery and feelings of success.

Torissa, a first-year teacher and graduate student from Indianapolis Teaching Fellows, shared these thoughts about modeling behavioral choices in our Saturday class a few months ago.

"One of my students was always posturing and reacting in anger to a correction or what I thought to be constructive criticism, which almost always landed her in a five-day school suspension. I reminded her over and over again that there are many ways to express how you feel that won't get you into trouble with the school and your parents." But then I noticed I was reacting and posturing the same ways my student was in times of conflict, or when I felt insecure or stifled by co-workers, students and colleagues. What I was observing with my student was present inside my own interactions and ways of dealing with dissension. Torissa kept encouraging her student, helping her to generate responses that revealed honesty and frustration, yet would not anger authority or show disrespect. Finally, the results of Torissa's efforts were enlightening for this particular young woman and for herself. By responding different-

ly, both Torissa and her student were able to experience a freedom, a way of expressing their feelings without the punitive consequences of past responses. It was truly a revelation and learning experience for teacher and student! Torissa demonstrated compassion. She modeled respect, assisting her in ways to generate and create various responses that would emotionally and socially serve her well in school and in the future.

How may I serve you? These are the words that can potentially turn a world upside down with well-being and gratitude. What would happen if we were to begin any day with an open heart and willingness to create prosperity in relationships inside the classroom **even** when we are shut down with nasty comments and inappropriate behaviors? Are we able to transcend the outer layers of undesirable conduct, knowing that those few words, "How may I serve you?" are able to create a constructive difference in a student or teacher's life? The positive effect of peeling back the layers of undesirable behaviors may not be immediately felt, but experienced at a later time, when student and teacher begin to feel generous movements in improved academic performance, social relationships and enhanced behaviors incited by a caring heart and a desire to assist another. What we know is that positive emotion directly affects the performance of the brain and working memory. When the alignment of emotion and intellect are activated, an innate intelligence is recovered and present—compassion. *Compassion for another* is not naïve or impossible; it is intelligence in the deepest sense. It is self-awareness and an alert knowing that we affect and are intimately connected to one another.

Fresh Perspective

All persons explain circumstances through the lenses of their own experiences. What we perceive as our reality may be completely different for another, depending on his/her beliefs and prior life experiences. When we truly begin to understand this notion, we respond to one another with hearts wide open. *Hearts wide open*—this phrase may sound trite, fluffy and confusing to many. Responding from the heart to this challenging reality we call *life* is unrealistic and unattainable, many might say. A "heart response" is **not** synonymous with sitting in a neutral or gray area agreeing with everyone and always accepting what is before us. A heart response calls us to *lead* with the heart, and when we lead with the heart, the mind follows. I once was told that a *hero* is one who hears the call of his life purpose and responds—not a doer of great deeds. I desire for students to know they are the heroes in life and act on this truth! As educators, it is our responsibility to turn up the volume inside our students' hearts so they can hear the music of their life purpose and voraciously respond.

Perspective drives all that we name, experience, and evaluate each moment of every day. As I write these notions, the children's book by Judith Viorst, *Alexander and the Terrible Horrible No Good Very Bad Day*, comes to mind. In this story, a young boy awakens to a 12-hour period during which every event, person, experience and thought perpetuates negative emotion this little boy has subconsciously held. We have all experienced similar days in which one moment of conflict and agitation is followed by a downpour of frustrating, annoying and aggravating circumstances. All people are able to slide into bouts of negative thinking and become entangled in rigid perspectives. Teachers have the great privilege of assisting children and young adults into forming broader perspectives where life's challenges do not feel so overwhelming. When a child or adolescent feels able, successful and worthy, there is no greater feeling for the student, parent or teacher.

The *arena of education* is the foundation for every facet of life: business, government, economics, medicine, law, and global dynamics. If we cannot assist our students in discovering an imaginative perspective that upholds a deepened understanding of purpose and self-awareness inside our preparation for real world relationships and experiences, then we are not teaching to full capacity. Just taking a singular experience and assisting one another to see the good in oneself and the outcome no one expected **is** teaching from the heart. We must align our thinking so that we begin to experience more positive moments. Young children are resilient, ripe for releasing unproductive perspectives that can chain adults to their circling negative thinking and repetitive and fruitless behaviors.

An integral aspect of teaching promotes self-acceptance and self-efficacy in relation to others. Plasticity of perspective is the key unlocking rigid and boxed-in conditions and cultures that permeate classrooms, hallways, and offices of those who choose to live and work in the world of educating children. The choice to teach is an excellent one. Yet, the conditions are deplorable for those who choose to see and experience its impenetrable lesions of conflict and division.

I choose to see a fresh and pliable perspective in the world of teaching and learning, one viewed through the heart, the inner source of our being. I choose to explore a view filled with the colors and designs of the imagination, serving student and teacher in creating *excellency* and *extravagance* in the educational process. This place is "the inner home." Home is where teachers, administrators, students, and parents sit beside one another contemplating the essential questions. Of course, there will be moments of conflict, but always followed with an understanding that transcends individual and systemic differences. It is the place of wonderment where the imagination and creative spirit are resurrected and the answers to life's questions are found within.

The Little Prince *comes to mind when he learned of the Fox's secret. "One sees clearly with only the heart; anything essential is invisible to the eyes."*

Teach for America, The New Teacher Project and other transition to teaching programs are training teachers across the nation to embrace high expectations, rigor, and content as "leaders" who know how to get the most from the students. Is it enough? There has been a movement toward college preparation in teacher training programs that will emphasize content and assessment for licensing requirements. This will lead to a lessened focus on educational pedagogy and theory. These could be enviable changes, but will they be enough to invoke engagement, purpose, and imagination, but more importantly, a placid relationship between teacher and student? I know that when a student is not feeling respected inside the classroom walls, he or she will not give a damn about the books placed on the desk or projects assigned with detailed rubrics. We will lose the heart of learning if we do not teach and model deep listening while sitting with the questions, traveling from the head to the heart while creating a balance of both.

Reflections from First Year Teachers
February 5, 2010

Hi Lori,

Here is my reflection covering the month of January. It was certainly an interesting month as it was my first time coming back after an extended break. I would say I was a bit surprised with how unsettled the students were when we returned from break. I will certainly take this into consideration in future years. I struggled with trying to figure out if I needed to be tougher or easier on them those first couple of weeks back.

I believe that I have already discussed my recent struggles with putting the upcoming standardized testing into perspective. It seems that we are spending so much time "teaching to the test." My other Marian class this semester is on assessment, and I have been really questioning why we give our students so many standardized tests throughout the year (NWEA three times, Acuity four times, ISTEP twice). While I am still in the early stages of developing my assessment philosophies, I really am starting to believe that I could make even greater gains with the students if they only had to take the ISTEP. I think that if I have strong assessment practices myself, that should negate the need for all of the additional testing the students do throughout the year. The various standardized testing disrupts classes, takes away from instruction time, and we have to work our tails off just to invest the students in being willing to take them seriously. The whole process really seems to go against doing what is best for the students and I see myself struggling with that reality into the future.

One of the huge revelations that I had this month was how truly behind many of my students are. Despite the huge gains I have already made, some of them still remain years behind grade level. They are in middle school or high school and still have significant trouble with simple mathematical calculations, short reading passages, and ultimately, the concept of how hard they have to work to really close their own achievement gap. I discuss with them regularly that I can teach my heart out, but I cannot learn FOR them. I mean, I know that I was put in a school like this for a reason and have built so much trust with my students. However, it breaks my heart to know that for them to really make significant gains and catch up to grade level, they are going to need teachers like me, year after year, from now until the end of high school. And they need so much more than that... more support at home; less absences; better nutrition; more role models; less focus on television, cell phones, iPods, and the internet; more after-school activities... the list goes on and on. I think I will really struggle with this so long as I am teaching students in high-poverty areas. I can only give so much and these kids need so much more than that. I can only hope that my presence in their life, short as it might be, will have a lasting impact on their desire to become the best person that they possibly can.

As far as my instruction goes, I am certainly planning to try more varied strategies as I finish out my first year of teaching. I am beginning to use more math manipulatives. I have taken your advice and have let the students do more work at the board, create quiz problems, and have started to make their academic progress in my class more transparent. I have also started to push the envelope a little bit from a rigor standpoint. I think some of my students started to become a bit bored with the material I covered last semester. I will not allow that to happen this semester. If anything, I want to make them a bit uncomfortable with the high expectations I am setting for them. I truly believe that these students will respond to a raised bar if they are pushed enough. As I am finding out, it takes a lot of pushing.

I am very much looking forward to next school year. Not that I am not focused on finishing this year strong, but I am especially excited about having the extra time over the summer to rework strategies, develop curriculum, and read up on some best practices. As we continue through this semester, please keep this in mind for my ongoing development. Time is scarce now for a significant amount of variety, but with some extra time over the summer I think I can further mold my growth as a premier educator. Please continue to send any and all suggestions my way... I may not implement them all "tomorrow," but I would like to implement a lot of them over time.

Your ongoing support is appreciated and I am looking forward to a great rest-of-the-semester.

Take care,
Tom

Relationships

How may I serve you? This is the question that sets fire to our hearts and desires to learn. This question ignites the probability of diffusing the frustration felt during unexpected moments when tempers flare and feelings of exasperation permeate the dialogue between teacher and student, teacher and teacher, teacher and administrator or parent and teacher.

Is education about relationships? Without hesitation, an emphatic yes! Relationships assist us in understanding ourselves and those around us. Inside schools, relationships provide a way to self-reflect, gauging who we are and where we are as we strive to reach our goals and dream the impossible. *There is not a child or adult that doesn't desire to be understood and loved. There are no techniques, behavioral strategies or assessments that provide the unique DNA for reaching out to students who dare you to teach them and educational leaders who dare you to change the ways of a broken system...* When asked, "How may I serve you?" we begin to trust and understand the space where teacher and student reflect within, seeing one another in the eyes of the other. Here in this place, the seeds are posited for mastery:

mastery of relationship, content, critical thinking and problem-solving spurred by our inbred curiosity and the power of a dormant but bubbling imagination. For when we serve another, we fill ourselves up in abundant ways. *How may I serve you?* This question sparks spiritual leadership. In the words of Neale Donald Walsch, author and spiritual leader:

> *You are invited by life to elect yourself a Spiritual*
> *Leader, and to take office today. What does a*
> *spiritual leader say? A spiritual leader does not say,*
> *"Follow me." A spiritual leader says, "I'll go first."*
> *Decide today to take the oath: I promise to "go first"*
> *in demonstrating forgiveness, compassion, understanding,*
> *generosity, kindness, cheerfulness, positivity, and love.*

Jonathon Kozol, author of *Letters to a Young Teacher*, responds to the relationship a young teacher has established with her students. He writes,

> The children had known you for only a month,
> but the chemistry had already set in. No curricu-
> lum, rules, standards, however good or wise they
> may appear, can substitute for this bond. This
> bond of trust and tenderness comes first. Without
> that, everything is else is dutiful—and generally
> deadening. It is not for dutiful aridity that people
> become teachers. 27

Fall 2009
Magnificent Teaching
Walter E. Nordstrom
Indianapolis Teaching Fellows

I received a phone call Friday from a student with an EH I had in my Speech and Journalism classes for four months. I teach in a residential facility, so my students come and go frequently. She was successfully discharged and now attends a public high school nearby. At one point in her residency, she had written a story she didn't intend for me to see. It encompassed the details of my demise at her hand. I found it and confronted her. It was a call for help and I recognized it as such. Instead of reacting with anger, I critiqued it and encouraged her to rewrite it and make it more effective. She didn't rewrite that story, but she did begin to put more effort into her writing in both of my classes. I continued to encourage her and point out the strengths in her writing. I was also able to get her to revise more willingly by approaching it from the stand-point of making something good into something great. She called me last Friday to let me know that she is on the newspaper and the yearbook at her new school. She also took second place in a news writing contest recently. This being the first call of this sort that I have ever received; I wasn't sure exactly how to react. So I was just honest with her and told her that I knew she could do whatever she put her mind to. I couldn't be more proud.

There are the teachers that teach of life journeys, reflection and compassion as an innate intelligence, an inherent part of their curriculum. They embrace a natural understanding in the face of adversity, seeing through the veils of unpleasant behaviors and hate-filled words. They remember the children, seeing their own successes and struggles in their students' eyes. Walt Nordstrom and Tom Hakim remembered this and learned much.

"How may I serve you?" Mr. Pickett inquired. He was learning the secret of teaching.

Who Are You?

One simply cannot step inside and change up the matrix of education without questioning who he/she is inside their personhood and in the role of teacher. We cannot modify assessments, intensify curriculum, differentiate instruction, and create legislation regulations without delving into these two questions.

Who are you that teaches?
Who are you that learns?

Self-reflection is a journey of the heart that must be taken seriously if we are to solidify a passion for teaching and learning once again. Paradox rests at the core of the teaching and learning process. When I declare a definitive truth about a teacher, student, or classroom environment, it is only my truth, quite possibly a story I have concocted based on my beliefs and experiences. It is one that can shift for various reasons, with time and experiences. If I am growing and evolving as both teacher and student, hopefully my perspectives will change.

Standing in front of 52 Teach for America teachers in my graduate class over two years ago, I made a decision and promise to myself and to them. I would willingly and joyfully take the roles of student and mentor. I promised to begin each class with a curiosity for content and instruction, but what I would hold close at all times was a desire to know myself and therefore each of them as we dove into the heart of educating our future world citizens. I try to embrace this curiosity and desire to self-reflect with each new semester and course or class. As educator and speaker Carol Tomlinson states, "Teaching is an organic process."

Observing the eyes of these young teachers who had been teaching in the inner city schools for five short months, I saw trepidation and some unexpressed fear, disguised in bravado. These young teachers were strongly motivated yet confused. They were confused by this paradoxical and cycling profession where test scores, assessment, data, legislation, and standard-based education appeared to drive their teaching, and this felt intrinsically wrong. I saw the eyes of servitude and compassion in these young teachers. They were hungry; not for theory, policies, or lists of ways to differentiate and assess instruction; they desired to make a difference in the lives of their students. They were told over and over again—high expectations, high expectations and higher expectations, but were these directives accurate, helpful, and enough? What happened along this singular one-dimensional mindset, this path that was intended to create the "right expectations"?

The questions flew from their mouths. "How do I keep from yelling at this student who walks in the door and immediately begins disrupting the class, tapping his pencil on everything except the paper? What do I do when a student turns to the class and shouts „Fuck you,' and then walks to his seat and slumps down?" These new teachers wanted solutions and "ways of being" with students that they could activate the next morning. They desired measurable and tangible ways to fix the problems so that the students could begin to learn. Fixing a problem is part of the problem. These teachers would soon begin to understand this...

Asking the questions and listening... Is it enough? Yes. Yes, a resounding yes! It is enough, because what is the student truly saying to the teacher when he is yelling, "Fuck you," or when she completely shuts down, pulling her hoodie over her head, or when he refuses to participate, shoving his book into his book bag or throwing it across the floor? What is the student saying to the teacher when he skips classes to smoke weed or is suspended for fighting for the third time in the first grading period? Could the student be saying, "I am not enough. I am just not enough"? I believe she is. Is it not our responsibility and honor within a compassionate curriculum to explore this self-defeatist attitude of unworthiness, unwrapping and exposing a truer view, one that sees the possibilities and latent talents?

The teacher walks over to the student and stands by his side. He gently places his hand on his student's shoulder. "What do you need? Please tell me." There is no response, only a swift pulling away and additional slumping. The teacher continues to envision this student at his very best and who he truly is, listening, intently listening... and patiently waiting. He waits for a few minutes, hours, and then it is tomorrow. "How may I serve you?" The student is still attending class but there is vacancy... no response from the outside, but what is going on in the inside, inside the heart and mind of this young adolescent? Do we really know? Weeks pass. There is a slight outward response. It is not a verbal response, but one that the teacher can feel in the center of his chest. Moment by moment and day by day the landscape is changing... The relationship is gathering trust, and the hearts of teacher and student are expanding. Oh, there are still days when "go to hell" is mumbled, desks are tipped over, books are thrown around, and hope feels lost, but those times are fewer. It is a process, an unending story that deserves to be put into words. Martin Luther King Jr. said:

Our goal is to create a beloved community, and this will require a qualitative change in our souls as well as a quantitative change in our lives.28

This is why I am creating and sharing a new story. A story that we have forgotten. Not because I have the tangible tools or am an expert in behavior management, collaboration, and best practices within the arena of education. And certainly not because I can fix what is wrong in any class or school. Quite the opposite; I am both student and teacher with a heightened awareness of the awaiting gifts inside each and every child, just as I see my own.

When I explore the darkness and the light of my own evolutionary being, I begin to slowly understand that of my students. How may I serve you?

From personal and professional experiences, I have learned that force, anger, and sarcasm only deepen the wounds when we communicate with children and adolescents. Until we meet a child with understanding and authenticity, we will rarely experience or see an intrinsic desire to learn or feel her excitement from a fresh discovery. Author and teacher Parker Palmer states,

> Teaching tugs at the heart, opens the heart, even breaks the heart—and the more one loves teaching, the more heartbreaking it can be. The courage to teach is the courage to keep one's heart open for the questions, the mystery, and in those very moments when the heart feels full to capacity. 29

When we inadvertently take the "soul" out of education, we are left with a skeletal caricature that distorts and diminishes the significance of the beating heart inside our classrooms. Education is much more than content acquisition and test scores. It is the vehicle that drives us to question, creates curiosity, and is able to bring us to an *understanding* about ourselves and the world around us. When we discover meaning and relevancy in our lives, the treasure of "heart" is uncovered, and purpose paves our path.

Brea Thomas, a graduate student and teacher of secondary students in Indianapolis, Indiana, shares these words of soulful teaching as she learns about herself each day through time spent with her students.

There is meaning in a hug—and hugs can be verbal, not just physical. This is what I've learned in my few years as a high school English teacher. This notion guides me as I maneuver through this hypersensitive time period in schools when even sideways hugs or complimentary pats on the back are scrutinized. Though there might be tremendous, and even necessary, restrictions on human caring, I like to challenge myself to address this idea of how to show students that we, teachers, really care, and that they, students, truly matter to us.

It sounds cheesy to us, perhaps, to say that "we care" or that "someone matters" because we're living in times of cynicism and distrust. I reflected on this dilemma last August as I began the year with multiple intelligence surveys and interpersonal activities to "get to know" my students.

How can I tell them, I brainstormed, without sounding cheesy, that their smiles and frowns matter; their puzzled and inquisitive brows matter; their sighs and chuckles and complaints—matter to me, and guide my daily teaching? Indeed, every caring teacher will consent to the fact that the verbals and nonverbals of her/his students get packed away and shuffled home, along with grading and lesson plans, to be analyzed and strategically reworked for the next day.

So, after issuing a three-page syllabus to my 11th Grade AP/IB Language students on Day 2 of last school year, following introductory exercises and "get to know you's" (as all teachers in our department are advised to do), I noticed that my students were flipping their noses and contorting their faces into the "I don't care—she must not care, either" look. So, I decided to write them a poem that would let them know how much I cared.

Night Letter to My Students

I jolt from slumber, and begin the day's ascent
A sprinter on the track,
A bloom reaching for the sun,

only to stand in my pjs
an ordinary teacher
enveloped by mini mountains of papers and books.

If I were eighteen, I might be pondering
the colors of my nail polish,
and the true meaning of the text message that my friend just sent me,

and the cruelty of a snooze button that won't last for eternity.
But as it is, I am simply awake,
a teacher in pjs, thought-full

still sensing your distress from the day before
and the furrowing of your brows
and the immensity of the accelerated tasks before us.

The apple cinnamon candles lull me forward
from slumber to coffee, from oatmeal to lunch-packing
and I rampage the kitchen to soothe the morning hunger mountains in my
belly.

iTunes have followed me out and down the porch steps
and humming them, I start the engine thinking
It's a Beautiful Day as Morning's Potential curls her lips into a smile.

The smell of my mums
waves good luck as I'm off to Our Garden

of classics and classes and clases de classicus…

and there's something about the street lights
torching against the darkness that makes me emboldened
to continue goading you to torch brightly, effervescently

but perhaps you aren't even listening

perhaps the droll or daunting of the day, of so many dreams
has you checked-out or singing a different tune—
specs of chalk dust, flecks of markers and pen ink

    and she wants us to have binders?

But this is
all that I want to do—
Tell you that in all of this…apples and dust, classics and classes…
    and binders
There is meaning, I promise.

                                   ~ Ms. Thomas

After reading this poem to my students, I noticed that some of them opened up—not, I believe, as a result of any poetic devices or exquisite linguistics, but because I opened up to them and made my caring transparent and personal. The rest of that initial week of school, I heard fewer moans and groans about books and early lessons, and I even received a few statements of appreciation from them.

So what did I learn from this fifteen minute homework exercise for myself, and the fifteen minutes that it took to share this simplistic poem with my students? I learned that caring for another is not a manufactured process or action. It is organic; it is a way of living and breathing each day, hoping for positive results from selfless efforts. This is serving; this is teaching.

This year, as I approach the first weeks of school again, I am smiling—looking forward to the new poem that I will create, and the new bridges that I'll be able to form with my students, which are centered on genuine caring and serving. I'm hoping that once again, I will smile as I see some of my students put the new poem in the front cover of the binders that they originally groaned about purchasing. Indeed, I'm thrilled that I've discovered that such small actions can yield welcomed rewards. It didn't cost me anything to open up to them, or to show my caring, and the teaching pay-offs were absolutely worth it.

Brea Thomas
Pike High School
Indianapolis, Indiana

Most children bask in a world of innocence and well-being until early adolescence. It is then the curtains of conditions and worldly expectations are met with narrowed scrutiny, societal values, peer evaluation, and often times disapproval. Cultural traditions and biases, tethered with human-generated rules and boundaries that didn't matter so much in early childhood, begin to complicate the process of inner wisdom and growing self-esteem. I once read that to muster understanding of the mindset and belief system of adolescents, we must know their unspoken motto, "Never embarrass me."

If we truly assign and attest to "Best Practices" as our model of pedagogy, then we must delve deep into the murky waters of child and adolescent development. It is here where questions, imagination and erratic emotional growth are developing and present, sometimes active and often times hidden with buried desires.

Where I begin with you, the reader, is a transition into story-telling, a type of envisioning and an imaginative scope that views the heart as the engine that drives change; a story that urges the heart into action with feeling and passion. Story-telling rests in the essence of who we are. It resonates in a place where the brain has difficulty reaching, but the imagination sets fire to our desires and potential. Creative imagination is our natural birthright, one that we have forgotten on this journey along education and life.

Raw Change

What is true is not always real and what is real is not always true.

We have transformed into a society where immediate responses, solutions and practical problem solving lay the groundwork for happy and successful lives. I have watched countless individuals who have attained external goals, reached esteem in the eyes of others, lived abundantly in the material world, and yet there seems to be an inner storm, an unrest swirling inside their hearts that no "thing" from the outside world is able to soothe or contribute to a peaceful sense of well-being. *It is an insurmountable and intricately complicated task to respond with advice or judgment when it comes to the underpinnings of a heart at war with itself...*

In Alice in Wonderland, *the Mad Hatter asked Alice, "What do a raven and a writing desk have in common?" She pondered the question throughout the story. At the end of her journey, preparing to go home, she posed the question back to the Mad Hatter. He smiled and said, "I don't really know, Alice." She grinned with satisfaction.*

What do a raven and a writing desk have in common? This question provides fodder for thought and a creative opening to many types of notions and reasons for the second half of this story. Must we always search for the correct and particular solution or the one right answer as our number two pencils frantically color in the little round circles, hoping for higher test score? Does this higher score and one right answer create professions and meaningful work in which our passions and interests are addressed, nurtured and challenged? Do the higher test scores and grade point averages foster meaningful relationships as we learn about one another?

The mystery of questions posed in story-telling and its symbolism can lead us to the answers and solutions we are looking for within the context of "what is" and what is to come inside our own lives. Story-telling explores meaning and purpose in our lives at a deeper level. It is inside the story where we begin to see beyond the disparity of achievement and fragmented behaviors in and out of the classroom. Seeds are positioned that have the propensity to carry us into realms of dreams *not* deferred, but fully realized. What is the story of your life? What is the story of your student's life, the one that pushes all your buttons and tempts you to feel angry, annoyed, uneasy and unsuccessful? What is the story of your colleague's life, your administrator's and neighbor's? Do we really know entering the relationship with compassionate understanding?

The *perspective* of turning the impossible into the possible has lost its magic and influence inside our schools and quite possibly our lives. We have forgotten that the courageous and *out of the box* thought processes of our great inventors, teachers, and leaders of the world were not considered normal, were not encouraged or accepted. What looked like defeat from the outside in was often times revered years later as an epic achievement from these aspiring individuals. And if those students of invention and imagination did become discouraged, they did not sit for long in a stagnant state of hopelessness. They pushed on. Not with reason, but with heart.

Placing our Imaginations and Creative Visions on the Table

Educators require the specific techniques and strategies, the tools that affect the learning and teaching process. The question is, are we leaving out the power of a story, a story shared? Stories persuade us in jumping outside our subjective perspectives, the small worlds in which we swim when troubling events occur or negative emotion reigns supreme. During stressful occasions our minds begin to summon, repeat and invent thoughts and solutions that may or may not be accurate. John Kotter, Harvard Business School professor and leading author on effective leadership, states,

> Over the years I have become convinced that we learn best—and change—from hearing stories that strike a chord within us. The dry academic tomes I wrote very early in my career were earnest reflections of the research I conducted, the analysis I applied and the conclusions I drew. And they had few readers, mostly other academics. I learned along the way and started including more and more stories in my work. My later books were read by many more people than my earliest work. As I look around today, I see that too few business leaders and administrators grasp the idea that metaphorical stories can have a profound effect on people. The gestures made (or not made) by leaders can turn into the stories that powerfully affect behavior. 30

Do we truly know one another's stories? Do we grasp the experiences our students and teachers have endured or the journeys they have traveled, linking their present reality in this very moment?

"You cannot hate anybody if you have walked in their shoes." *What is their story? What occurrences and experiences do they bring to school? How do we respond when we understand?* This is the revolutionary perspective that is the *work* of education, *compassionate presence, driven with inquiry.* A philosophy that we cannot ignore or neglect!

In the next section of this book, I hope you will ponder and pull from this story the meaning that inspires and creates hope inside your own life. It is this type of exploration and discovery bound in *questions* and *concepts* that begins the process of effective and deepened teaching and learning in schools, homes, and businesses across the world. A malleable heart and desire to expand self-knowledge and a deepened understanding of one another is the impetus for our new archetype of teaching and learning. Our schools are sorely missing this component today, but there are many educators and parents who are remembering to restore the infallible fabric of *relational education,* spurring the intuitive wisdom, ready and able to express itself in those genius students, parents and educators who are doing their best and have not forgotten, all is well.

Research repeatedly reports students intimately learn and retain subject matter when it is formatted into stories. This is where I begin: within the imagination, where we all once gathered with confidence and curiosity as we listened to that intuitive, all-knowing teacher, the heart. Questions about our future are bubbling with possibility as we explore and ask ourselves, *Who am I? What is my purpose? What is the purpose of life? Who am I that teaches? What can I create? Why am I teaching? Who are my students?* Stories assist us in understanding the authorship of our lives.

If *Best Practice* is to model, demonstrate and integrate rather than reporting and lecturing what is to be learned, then the following section of this book could be looked upon as a "strategy." This section embraces a story-telling methodology combining creative visualization, prediction and experiential design. I encourage you to embrace the constructs of change, envisioning what education could look like in future days. What did Martin Luther King envision and therefore create before it became a working reality? He imagined a positive movement in which equity and respect for individual differences, no matter the color of skin, became the life and breath of this country. What did Walt Disney envision, and how did he use the imagination to create the kingdom of enjoyment so many millions of people visit today? He imagined and believed in the possibilities of change and growth that would bring immense pleasure to millions of people.

Inside this educational prototype we cannot afford **not** *to imagine the possibilities, the visions and hope for happier, successful and holistically healthier educators, parents, and students.*

Part Two

A New Snapshot

What would it feel like to be a first-year teacher in this time of new national core standards integrating compassion alongside specialized content integrated into the national curriculum? I have envisioned a middle school similar to the schools I visit today when observing and supervising my first- and second-year teachers from Teach for America and the New Teacher Project. The character of Gabe typifies and is a collective persona of the young first- and second-year teachers that are presently teaching or are preparing for work in the inner city and public charter schools in Indianapolis, Indiana.

My vision of school leadership is embraced inside the words, gestures and behaviors of Catherine. Although the name has changed, this young woman represents "leadership" in its finest moment. This leadership embraces ferocity of heart and mind. Her attention to students and parents is incredibly powerful and focused as she integrates a holistic perspective from the top down, and paradoxically, from the bottom up. Haven Middle School is similar in size and function to many large public middle schools today, and through collective optimism and imagination, this section of the story reveals the possibilities inside a new era of teaching and learning in public education. If we are to model the changes we require from one another, then creating a story, envisioning what is desired, is best educational practice.

In the years ahead, I envision an international league of retired, veteran and new educators and parents trained in mindful learning, a methodology that encompasses focused attention as its end goal with an emphasis on perspective, thought formation and applied empathy highlighted in relational learning. The Fellowship of Sages could assist teachers and students in connecting the power of emotion and thought to the enhancement of core standards and content through a student's prior knowledge base, personal beliefs and cultural heritage. This fellowship of teachers will mentor educators and students towards the unification of relevant, rigorous, and meaningful curriculum intermixed with the intelligence of the heart—serving one another with gratitude and a deepened self-awareness.

I envision exceptional educational leaders such as Parker Palmer, Jenifer Fox, John Taylor Gatto, Jonathon Kozol, Eric Jensen, Marilee Sprenger, Rick Lavoie, Tal Ben-Shahar, Judy Willis, and Dan Seigel, among others, escorting the Fellowship of Sages across this nation and world as teachers embrace a novel way of shifting the notions of schooling into an extravagant model of mindful, brain-based, and holistic education led by a compassionate presence.

First Year of Teaching, 2012

First Day of School

Hunched over the rickety family heirloom, a three-legged ice cream table exhausted and breaking down from supporting conversations and intimate diatribes through the years, Gabe's chameleon disposition repeated the question as he sipped his lukewarm coffee. *What am I doing?* The inquiry hung in the air suspended inside a bubble, refusing to pop as it steadily filled the small cubicle of a kitchen with its abrupt descent of timing and readiness. Setting down his mug, he rubbed his forehead and closed his eyes. He knew the next logical step—teaching. He would deeply listen, as he had so many years ago, to that place that appeared to serve him well in the end: his heart.

A twenty-seven-year-old man and several members of his teaching cohort, the *Fellowship of Sages*, had been unexpectedly called by the administration and then placed inside the nucleus of the crisis—a chaos and calamity that was brewing in the aftermath of state and national educational reform. Gabe had prepared for the profession that lay before him. He was a teacher, intricately trained in one of the most esteemed schools of education in the country.

He didn't look or act much like a typical teacher. Built lanky and lean like his mother, he tolerated curly blonde hair that hung to his shoulders in tight, frizzy ringlets. Through the years, a brush or comb had greeted those curls maybe five or six times. He was grateful for this innate convenience, and if he were brutally honest, he rather enjoyed his physical appearance, although the small brown mole on the lower side of his left cheek bugged the hell out of him. His friends and even strangers told him it was his mark of distinction, attractive, but he thought that crap, although it was there to stay, as he had sworn to himself he would never set foot in a doctor's office or hospital unless he was painfully near death.

Gabe loved sports, mostly basketball. He didn't care to sit for hours on end watching and commentating or listening to ignorant opinions—but he played the game. He read the papers, magazines, any factual basketball genre he could get his hands on, memorizing detailed stats. He researched what he discussed. His dad always reminded him, "Don't shoot your mouth off to hear your own voice. If you are going to take a stand, you better know what the hell you're talking about... no one cares or desires to be around the armchair quarterback on any subject, Gabe." He heeded this advice even as a young boy, taking to heart the perspective and presented facts on any subject, analyzing for clarity and fodder in case of upcoming debates or discussions. Gabe had evolved into one hell of a listener, and this skill would prove to be crucial through his careers and life.

Gabe also loved unfiltered Camel cigarettes. Curiously, he realized basketball didn't mix well with this indelible habit, as he had tried numerous times to quit. When his anxiety heightened, the pack of Camels would slither their way off the top shelf, landing in his left hand. Why he went to the trouble of placing them in such a secretive place he could not understand, laughing at his own tormented confusion, though he begrudgingly continued taking that long, delectable inhale.

But in recent years, his love for kids had even surpassed his time and fervor on the courts and craze for smoking. He was drawn to the kids at the community center, filing in long lines every summer from the inner city schools where he had mentored a youth camp during the past few summer breaks. These kids were the ones struggling in life. Or were they? Another question he pondered, because he had learned a hell of a lot about life from these scrappy and street savvy kids and teens. It was a question he asked himself often: Who were the teachers?

Gabe's passion for their innocence, street sense, and authenticity heightened as he shared and wrote about these experiences on Monday evenings with his peers at the Fellowship meetings. As far as he was concerned, these meetings on Mondays motivated him more than most events. The Fellowship of Sages was a growing cadre of active and retired teachers, administrators, and parents. They shared their memories, research and anecdotes from years in classrooms, exploring and connecting to their students' hearts—*backwards planning, or from the inside out.* This is how the mind and brain were created to learn!

The Fellowship knew well the importance of rigor and content, but they understood balance. They recognized that for affirmative change in knowledge acquisition to take hold, teachers and parents would need to constantly envision "what was going well" in the lives of their children and students. The Fellowship wrote of their students' strengths, challenges, and desires for the future, but more notably, they shared stories of *joining hearts.* They wrote of their greatest teachers, their students, the *change agents* in education.

Gabe was the grandson of one of the initial members of the Fellowship. His grandfather, Mr. Eden, had taught middle and high school students for over forty years. A few years back, his wealth of wisdom and love of teaching had been discovered in over fifty rumpled and coffee-stained notebooks buried and locked in an old cedar chest in the family's attic. Of course, these were just samplings of all he had written and previously shared with thousands of educators through the years, but the notions written in these notebooks would serve many through Gabe's perspective in future days and ways not seen—just yet.

"How may I serve you?" The words played through Gabe's head as he showered and readied for the first day of staff preparation and meetings with parents. Haven Middle School housed an eclectic mix of students from far-reaching inner city and a few suburban areas. Gabe's close friend and cohort from the Fellowship, Catherine, had described the school landscape as a miniature New York City, and from what he had observed thus far, he agreed with this rudimentary analogy.

As his thoughts traced, etching the landscape of this new day in a strange school, panicking, he noticed the time and leapt out of the shower. He could feel the adrenaline of anticipation coursing through his blood at the prospect of teaching for the first time. Looking in the mirror, he noticed his reflection appeared wiser and much older than he recalled, and this view *startled the hell out of him*. "I look exhausted," he thought, stalking the stranger in the mirror.

Gabe's penetrating blue eyes and long lashes had carried him to and through every woman's heart for as long as he could remember. The deep clarity his eyes communed never gave way to his posited secrets to those who knew him well, except for Catherine. God, the way she could make him feel. He shook the loose blonde curls dry, noticing the fine lines tracing the almond shapes, while the dark shadows beneath the blue stared back at him. What the hell? He was riding a carousel of emotions, and he desperately needed to focus.

Attempting to shave with the battered razor, his thoughts managed to shift to Mr. Eden, his grandfather. Well-being, change, gratitude—he'd thought it bullshit at the time... but there was something about their presence, these wise and veteran teachers, parents and leaders sharing their humble experiences and authentic desires in hopes of improving a fragmented system. Their words echoed in his head, tugging on his heart and thoughts this morning.

Damn it, he'd sliced the side of his chin, and the cut would not stop bleeding. Sticking a wad of toilet paper on it, he hurried to the closet and pulled on his trusted torn jeans and black polo. Gabe grabbed his mug of coffee and gulped the last of the cold, bitter liquid, desperately needing the caffeine rush. Snatching his keys off the counter, he headed for the unknown... He just hoped the Ford Explorer would start, as its 190,000 miles had more issues and drama than his own young life. Lately, every time he started the truck it would gurgle, spit and sound as if its insides would explode, leaving him in the center of a smoke-filled metal fireworks show. Right now, he just didn't have the money to repair whatever the hell was wrong with it.

Staff Gathering: What Would We Say? What Would We Hear?

Haven, like many large public middle schools, held a steady enrollment of over 1500 students in three grades, and Gabe was keenly aware that several teachers and administrators were new to the district and schools. Pulling into the freshly paved parking lot, he found the corner space neatly bordered by bright yellow lines, where he wedged the truck into its new daytime home. "A new beginning for both of us," Gabe said out loud as he patted the dusty dashboard, opened the door, and hit the lock button.

The Fellowship of Sages, who were mentoring new teachers in this time, expecting a smooth opening to the school year, spoke of the right expectations when they congregated in the meeting halls and homes of one another, discussing ways to build relationships with their young scholars while enriching the learning environment. Emphasizing service to another within a curriculum designed to form and ask critical questions was paramount in their minds and teaching practices. Their questions delved beyond the trenches of standards and benchmarks, creating experiences or learning episodes that the students needed and desired.

Catherine, schooled at the university and mentored by the Fellowship, had been appointed as the new administrator at Haven. She would have her hands full with many novel tasks, especially the undertaking of bridging the emotional and academic gaps of new and veteran teachers. It certainly would require patience and some time. She was a natural at leadership subtleties, modeling and presenting a great combination of collaboration, while creating equanimity of teacher and student relations intermingled with compassion. She realized that successful educational reform would need to be a steady incremental improvement over time, and it would find success from the bottom up, one school at a time. She also anticipated that the integration of the core standard *compassionate presence* would be met with dissension and frustration, which, she bemused, would be great practice and modeling for herself, the students and all the staff.

Many of Catherine's notions were already being implemented inside schools in Japan. *Lesson Research Studies* were an integral part of teacher preparation and collaboration within many schools in this region. Beginning at Haven this fall, groups of teachers planned to work on improving teaching methodologies and student performance by taking a critical look at what was working well and what aspects of teacher performance and relational learning were lagging behind. Were they connecting to their students? *Emotional connection* seemed to be the missing link in implementing effective instruction with transference into problem-solving and critical thinking skills.

Lesson Research Studies were identified as "challenges" that posed dilemmas for students and teachers. The Lesson Research Studies were converted into demonstrated plans of action, actual lessons educators taught and modeled for one another in hopes of gleaning immediate and constructive feedback and reflection for implementation with their students. The reflections from these practice lessons were invaluable teaching aids for mastery of content. The design and differentiation that the teachers agreed upon would be implemented in the classrooms.

The focus of lessons was based on the timeless model of Abraham Maslow's hierarchy of needs. The teachers would examine and explore the primary and secondary needs with individual students as they determined the source of motivation for success inside instruction. The staff at Haven Middle School was beginning to understand that every human on the planet was motivated. Motivation was an innate human characteristic, but discovering the source of motivation was an entirely different issue. The focus of the research studies would be objective and positive, never focusing on teacher or student shortcomings and weaknesses. These studies would build on standards, but more importantly, they were designed to be emotionally appealing, motivating and meaningful to both teacher and student, continually building on the educator's and student's strengths and past knowledge.

During the initial staff meeting, Catherine was appropriately coy as her questions and explanations generated responses, unveiling desired alliances where potential disagreements and conflict started to brew. Somehow she coined an effective leadership approach and was intuitively prescient with regard to these skills. This leadership strength had followed her through high school and college, and more recently into the Fellowship and now inside Haven. Her proficiency would be tested, but she welcomed feedback; actually, she was fascinated by contrast and the thoughts of those around her. She knew too well she wasn't the expert.

Catherine's definition of leadership was hard to define or describe. She listened. She plodded through what she asked of others, but mostly her presence was noted in everything she embraced. She was a quiet, perceptive leader who understood the power of the ego and its limiting vices, although her temper could flare with those she trusted in unexpected moments. Gabe knew this well, as he was one of just a few recipients of these sometimes childish blow-ups. A paradox she was, living by these words she kept on her desk in her office and on the nightstand by her bed.

*You are invited by life to elect yourself a Spiritual
Leader, and to take office today. What does a
Spiritual leader say? A spiritual leader does not say,
"Follow me." A spiritual leader says, "I'll go first."
Decide today to take the oath: I promise to "go first"
in demonstrating forgiveness, compassion, understanding,
generosity, kindness, cheerfulness, positivity, and love.*

~ *Neale Donald Walsch*

The staff, parents and students at Haven gathered and began preparing for a new way of teaching. *They were preparing to meet one another where they were, building on one another's strengths and passions.* The staff didn't realize the enormous and powerful effects of this dialogue and assembly on this humid August morning. It would be remembered by many as a time of impartiality and delicate but powerful choices inside the hearts of those readying to teach and learn. The school, students, parents and staff would begin modeling service to another; a best practice that would create and tell a different story, one the world was ready to hear.

Collaboration or Egos Colliding?

I envision an administrator, an effective educational leader as Catherine, who leads with an instinctive knowledge that all persons are making choices, some consciously, others subconsciously, for the betterment of a systemic organization and doing their best in that very moment of operation.

Catherine was tall and slender, but her presence on this Monday morning was striking as she greeted all who walked through the wooden doors in preparation for the weeks and months ahead. Her large dark eyes scanned and reflected a raw hope of the gathering of all who chose to be a part of this new era. She saw eyes hesitantly waiting for some kind of preliminary leadership and direction.

Catherine walked to the podium and took a noticeable breath. Folding her hands, she began to speak. Gabe watched her squeeze her fingers so tightly in the clasped position that he could see the blood in a few of her fingers slide to the tips in the latched posture. She squeezed her hands in this way every time her heart and head worked in unison, emphasizing a thought or idea she felt most significant. It was a habit he had grown to love and one the Fellowship teased her about incessantly.

Words of Encouragement

"Good morning. I have much to share and an eagerness to hear from you." Already, Catherine's hands were flailing through the air with each expressed thought. So often, she reminded Gabe of his dad, as she always spoke her mind with a thousand hand gestures as if she were signing every time she spoke, maybe because it felt necessary in her mind to synonymously gesture while sharing her feelings for undeniable clarity. Gabe smiled as he thought she would never suffer from an illness brought on by repression—that was for sure.

"The question that keeps running through my mind is—what can I do for each of you in the upcoming months? I want you to think about how I can assist you in the process of teaching as we begin today with many questions and thoughts, but feelings churning in our hearts about how to create a place where learning is effortless, challenging and pleasurable. There is not a single teacher or parent or especially student that is ill equipped for this responsibility of the journey ahead. We have all that we need—but we must listen to our hearts and heads." She pointed to each place as she spoke. "Isn't it always about balance?" Catherine walked over to the side of the podium.

"In our formal training we learned of assessments, accountability, teacher leadership, literacy, differentiation, wrapping up our standards, sort of swathing them in ways to meet mandates set forth by state and national governments. We were focused on the mechanics of a curriculum and innovative technological advances, never imagining the circumstances or events that would propel each of us into a new position and so quickly." Heads nodded around the room as Catherine continued.

"I don't desire a broadcast of morning announcements or pronouncements that have alternate students reading a character pledge while their 1499 classmates are snickering at their seats because they know what this pledge is; a must-heard platitude demonstrating a collective ethical statement that feels meaningless to them and to us, if we are honest. I do not desire a separate curriculum on emotional literacy, role-playing empty banalities within scenarios—while discussing think sheets in the counselor's or dean's office. What we ask and expect from our students, we should be ready to match.

"It is time go within, observing how we feel and what we desire and will enjoy learning and offering. Our relationships with students and parents cement the foundation for growth in relational and academic learning, and really, isn't this about living life? We need to begin to understand this as an integral part of the curriculum. This is going to feel uncomfortable to some of you, and I do not desire a response, just your pondering of this question. Do you feel creativity is as important as literacy?" She hesitated. "Do we combine both so that student mastery and success of content, while understanding purpose, reaches new heights?

"In less than an hour the teachers, parents and students will break into smaller groups and begin to design instructional and behavioral plans implementing a compassionate standard with the guidelines you were given over the summer. We will listen to one another, taking notes and supplying information that has been left out or neglected in past years, knowing that these action plans are preliminary and a starting place for all of us as begin to teach and learn."

Again, heads nodded, comments were whispered, yet all were attentive to these opening words and notions. Looking down, Catherine examined her hands and then tucked the long dark strands of hair behind her ears. She came around the platform and looked out at the many expressions and eyes holding questions, anticipating her next few words.

"Gandhi stated that „we need to be the change we want to see in the world,' but I think there is much more to be explored from these words…" She hesitated and Gabe caught her eyes for just a split second. He found his hands in the clasped position, squeezing them so hard that the blood ran from his intertwined hands to the tips of his fingers. Looking down, he just shook his head, grinning.

Catherine continued…

"I think that if we consistently envision the inner strength of our students and their hearts, bringing this notion and these feelings to their attention each time we think and feel it, we will have created effective emotional mastery before textbooks open. Isn't this the place where learning begins? I believe we will observe improvement in academics and behavior because we will try… making an effort while allowing the students to venture along their own path. This is an essential part of the teaching and learning process.

"We cannot change the thinking of a government, an entire school system, or for that matter, the person sitting next to us, but we can focus on finding a perspective that holds our thoughts about ourselves and our students with strength of purpose and fiery potential. We have the control and direction in how we choose to respond in any situation."

There was some squirming and looks of confusion from the rows of teachers and parents—but Catherine's words floated in mid-air, patiently waiting for understanding, or maybe just acceptance at this point.

" I want to ask all of you some questions today for reflection and discussion, as I have pondered these myself over the last few days, feeling they are worthy of our exploration."

Teaching and Learning—A Journey of the Human Spirit

Catherine sipped her water, hesitated for what seemed to be an uncomfortable amount of time, then spoke:

"When we look past this grain of sand, which for the moment is Haven Middle School, sitting in the dead center of a swiftly changing global educational paradigm, is it not our goal to create a place for students to join together, setting a tone and an environment for peace-filled resolutions and purpose in and out of the classroom? How do we do this? I believe it begins with a five- or six-word question. When we ask, „What can I do for you?' there is a desire on the recipient's end to open to some notions that maybe would not have been heard or accepted when defenses were raised as minds closed—frantically searching for the right solution or correct response.

"As we collaborate with our Asian neighbors inside this illusion of competition, who is better prepared and taught, the United States or Japan, China or Japan, India or China, the United States or China, the United States or India? Have schools around the world in recent decades formed identities holding captive a limitation of creative mind and intuitive notions, trading these for robotic, sequential, competitive, and scientific approaches to teaching and learning, and therefore thinking? Is there room for both? Isn't education about relationships, dialogue and matters of the head and heart? Do scientists embrace matters of the heart? I believe the answers to these questions are yes, and scientists work from the balance of head and heart, because that is what keeps them moving from one perspective of a „failed research study' to another. Isn't success discovered inside the perspective of failing?

"Have we become extremists in matters of the head, the 60,000 or more thoughts a day which stir up the profundity of scholarly attainment, therefore starving the soul of wonderment and passionate vision? Although these questions might feel impersonal or irrelevant, what do they have to do with each of us individually? How can these questions directly influence our percolating minds and hearts within the context of education?"

Opening a book, Catherine recited the words of Jonathon Kozol, longtime author and educator:

> "The hidden curriculum is the teacher's own integrity and lived conviction. The most memorable lesson is not what is written by the student on a sheet of yellow lined paper; nor is it the clumsy sentence published (and 'illustrated') in the standard and official text. It is the message that is written in a teacher's eyes throughout the course of his or her career. It is the lesson which endures a lifetime. [31]

"Have we created and embraced a neurosis in which our students are feeling stifled and unmotivated within a structure that beyond a doubt carries the sizzling potential for change and growth? Again I believe the answer is yes. Can we become attentive to the new story, not just changing its characters and setting, but shifting its purpose and plot? I believe we can. Are we willing to put aside our perceived expertise and egos, our competing tendencies toward one another, readying ourselves to **listen** to the story of another—driving the subject matter and learning edges to new emotional and academic heights and realms?"

The room was hushed, and only the air conditioner's rattling gave way to the quiet as it droned the heat directly out of the room.

"I am ready to listen. I will begin by sitting next to each of you as you play with these changes—and I mean play with them ... enjoy these next few weeks and months as we create contrast, getting to know ourselves, one another and especially our students for the first time." Catherine looked down and stared into the eyes of the teachers and parents. "How may I serve you? How may I serve you in this new story? Can we create a place for our students to imagine and create from within—within the space of their genius capacity to understand?"

Catherine walked over to an empty chair. Her thoughts lagged behind, swirling in a world that was far removed from this gathering of eager parents, students and educators. Her eyes filled with tears. These tears signified change, not sadness or joyfulness, but they seemed to be indicative of an opening perspective that was challenging her comfort levels. No one spoke for a few seconds or maybe longer, as all seemed contemplative, taking notes and simply digesting the initial questions and notions. It was evident that Catherine was setting the tone for a compassionate, student-driven environment. But mostly, one of service and novelty, in which teacher and student together created and studied the questions, affirming all their contributions with respect for the thought processes of one another.

Delve In...

In this new time, educators, parents, and students were given two books to read and discuss. *A Whole New Mind*, by Daniel Pink, would be the launching pad for academic and relationship growth during the school year. Drawing on research from around the world, Daniel Pink describes the six aptitudes needed within this time of paramount movement as society moves from the Age of Information to the Conceptual Age.32 Design, story, symphony, empathy, play and meaning would be the spokes on the educational wheel; while the hub of *service to another* begins to drive the teaching and learning process through novel incremental and measurable changes.

The Alchemist, written by Paulo Coelho, was the second book chosen for the school's readings. It embraces the story of a young man's existential journey as a shepherd in a faraway land. Discovering the purposes of life and relationships with people, Santiago travels with his sheep, two stones, and a heart and mind latent with enthusiasm as he searches for his treasure, discovering the treasure to be closer than he ever could have imagined. Conjoined book studies with parents, educators and students taking turns leading discussions would assist in building the foundation for collaborative preparation, initiating assessment, designing classroom culture and self-empowerment within schools and homes. These studies would be an integral part of literacy, life purpose, and a central aspect of the Individual Learning Plans.

Mind Brain Education, research-based teaching strategies from Eric Jensen, Judy Willis, Robin Fogarty, and David Sousa, among others, would drive the instructional practices, assessments and service projects inside this urban middle school.

Community Leadership and Student-Led Learning

The Fellowship of Sages, retired and veteran teachers, administrators and parents, recalled when students feel safe and empowered within the classroom, they become intrigued and excited about the subject matter. Their role in the learning and assessment processes is self-activated with questions, healthy skepticism and commitment. Young brains are wired for excitement and learning, but also with an appropriate dose of developmental distraction, impulsivity and excitability. Waiting for a nine-week report card, the results of a unit test, or a parent-teacher conference is painfully difficult for most students. It is their innate birthright to be impulsive in moments. Waiting for long periods of time for the results and outcomes of their best efforts is grossly unfair. Waiting for teacher feedback is equally difficult and stressful in this technologically savvy time of quick responses. **Immediate and constructive feedback and reflection will** become a working and vital brain-based strategy in this new time of teaching and learning.

The teachers learned the importance of immediate and relevant feedback and its direct implication for *relational learning*. Used in isolation, standardized test results and nine-week, acuity, and end-of-course assessments, coupled with parent-teacher conferences, were antiquated assessments, leaving out the strength and purpose of students' insight and knowledge of what was needed and understood. The novel delivery of immediate and relevant feedback of assignments and projects generated a growing trust of content and a renewed confidence within teacher-student relationships.

The Fellowship of Sages discussed another key implication of the teaching and learning process—the power of relationship and trust created when teachers provide purposeful reflection and responses to students' work, efforts and attitudes—their own and their students.' In this new time of teaching and learning, the students' self-assessed much of their work alongside their peers. The educators followed suit. The teachers and parents were asked to self-reflect on their educational views, dispositions and contributions.

In this new era, the *process* of teaching was the engine for change... changes in behaviors, study skills, assessments, instruction and a desire to enact a *flow* through assignments and projects, cultivating a curiosity for learning. Brainstorming and mind mapping an array of solutions and explanations set learning on fire! Educators began to recognize the significance of a student's prior life experiences, cultures and belief systems inside the discussion of every academic subject. Students, on the other hand, learned quickly, became enthused and attached meaning and relevancy from their repertoire of **prior knowledge**. Interest inventories and individual surveys revealing student's histories, strengths, aptitudes and desires were a vital part of Individualized Learning Plans.

On the new national standardized tests, students were given questions based upon their prior experiences, cultures, aptitudes and passions. They were able to express their responses in a variety of ways. There were assessments of content and presented standards posed to inform instruction, increasing student capacity and mastery. However, the emphasis of the assessments was interspersed with students being asked to critically think through a challenge or enlisting assistance in the midst of a dilemma based on their heritage, experiences and culture.

A Teaching Heart in Years to Come
Fall 2012

"A service curriculum" was developing in urban schools around the country, but Haven Middle School was ahead of the game. This middle school was actively shifting perspectives based on conversations and a leadership that listened. There were no *strategic plans or reformed political mandate* filled with bullet points, a scattering of techniques and state directives. One school at a time felt the gentle effects of compassion and service as teachers, students and administrators relaxed into patterns of broadened perspectives while creating positive social experiences. There was a renewed focus on student and educator commonalities rather than differences. Leadership teams developed and began to integrate two to three-minute activities in which students, parents and teachers shared their histories, experiences and vulnerabilities.

Educators now understood the role of how **stress** affects school performance. Students' oppositional and impulsive behaviors were understood as the outward symptoms of those who were feeling pinched off from positive emotion and well-being.

Teachers understood that the negative behaviors spoke of a hidden adolescent belief, "I am not enough." Teachers began to envision, empathizing and therefore understanding how acute stress impaired learning and social skills, literally damaging neural connections, sometimes cutting the production of neurons in half.

The "work of education" became more enjoyable because there was an acceptance of the root of negative behaviors that had been absent in schools for so many years. The student's brain was looked upon as a mystery rather than a problem to be solved. If life is to be enjoyed, is not education? A working model of peaceful coexistence between colleagues, administration, parents and students took hold, highlighting strengths and assets, not weaknesses and shortcomings, as learning and instruction flourished. There was plenty of constructive criticism from teacher and student, but it was ushered in and out by frequent and positive feedback amongst all educators and students.

Who are the parents in this new time of Education Revelation? I envision them to be revered and uplifted no matter their dispositions, status, or contributions…

In this time, parents were *revered* for their contributions and presence inside schools. Their lack of presence and contributions didn't deter schools from consistently opening their doors, welcoming all. Educators recognized that fear and other obstacles contributed to parents' reluctance to be involved in schools, lessening their judgments and creatively discovering ways to partner with them. Periodic recognition nights were held, awarding all parents or guardians for supporting education in these times of change. Even if parents, grandparents or relatives were noncompliant or absent, they were gently encouraged to attend and participate in their student's educational journey through the Internet, via the web cam.

Educators began to keep their eyes on what they desired to see with regard to parent relationships, not what was actually occurring. The amazing facet of this type of visioning probability is that when we envision the best in anyone, we begin to see shifts and movements in a positive direction inside that individual's life.

But change is slow, and comfortable ways of doing become mindless and are not extinguished overnight. Parents of secondary students began to experience slight changes in the minds and hearts of their young adolescents towards school, as relationships were nurtured and students became increasingly curious. Scheduled and periodic home visits and mutually agreed upon phone calls calibrated considerable parent input into the process of the Individualized Learning Plans. As parents discovered that their input and assessment greatly mattered to teachers and the schools, they became willing and vital participants within the education process.

The national educational platform created programs and incentives for "service days" held monthly, inviting parents to attend school outings, work from home on school projects, or participate in any way that benefitted the students and teachers. Local businesses, organizations and mental health agencies shared in this community endeavor, offering a list of choices to serve alongside students, renewing a community connection with schools. Parents were financially compensated for service days. Community businesses were invited to participate several times during the school year. Parents and educators explored, discussed and chose particular businesses and organizations that would welcome educational involvement and student participation.

At Haven Middle School, students began to desire to know their teachers as persons. This desire grew more out of curiosity but became a necessary element of a budding relationship. From the students' viewpoints, teachers became people with feelings and aspirations. There appeared to be a growing and poignant respect for one another accompanying the delivery and integration of instruction. Teachers and students collaborated and questioned one another with deference rather than in mockery, disrespect or contempt. Educators, parents and students held each other accountable for closing achievement gaps, teaching to strengths and applauding one another's diversity in assessment and instruction. If students had questions, they were encouraged and expected to inquire.

Intentions—What Are They?

Intentions are larger in scope than learning outcomes, benchmarks or student goals. Educators, families and business leaders gathered quarterly, exploring and modifying the students' Individual Learning Plans. This program was deliberately piloted in the district's middle schools. Developmentally, this was a magical and sometimes risky transitioning time when young adults were questioning their identity, role and purpose in life. The students were dying to childhood and birthing an adulthood that was extremely underdeveloped. Adolescence is a time of great growth and confusion for many students, educators and parents.

Stated intentions were a significant facet of instruction and assessment. An intention was explained as a vision—a creative design connecting learning to real world experiences. Families, business leaders and educators were encouraged to brainstorm intentions with students based on interests, passions, strengths and aptitudes. The intentions were aligned with each student's current life purpose. From the statements of intentionality, the students were encouraged to create mind maps, designing instruction across subject areas. Teachers, parents and students constructed plans of action accompanied with significant practice steps, coupled with thought exercises that would generate alternative ideas in creating their visions and curriculum maps. The rigor of these intentions exceeded academic goals and objectives. They encompassed a process of envisioning the possible with a no-fail policy. Students were encouraged to look at the **"what if"** instead of the **"what is"** in their life experiences in and out of school. The intentions were met with a multitude of viable options, generating a mutual effort and a hearty communication process between teachers and students.

Brent Cameron, educator and author of Self Design, a methodology and practice based on the belief that children are natural learners and that the brain is designed for relationship, innovation and creativity, spearheaded the Individualized Learning Plan Initiative, merging the philosophy of Self Design into many districts from urban schools. Brent describes the process of Self Design in the following way: "It is a journey back to our true identity, allowing the rediscovery of self, the rediscovery of our essential nature. Can we recapture a sense of authoring our own lives, of using our self-authority to design our world as we wish it to be?" 33 Using the promise of authorship and building on students' strengths and interests, below are a few of the topics of intentionality that students, families, and educators created based on their creative visualization process. Their hope was that these topics would be discussed, formatted and implemented someday as **National Core Teaching Standards.**

Intentions/Topics created for Individual Learning Plans and the future formation of National Standards in Education

1. Environment—how do we affect, treat and stay in sync with our natural resources, promoting growth and an emergence of compassion towards the organic world we inhabit, increasing economic growth and commerce?

2. How do we play with mathematical concepts, expanding these skills into applicable professions of science, engineering and finance, formulating problems while creating solutions inside global markets?

3. Creative writing and reading is a component of entrepreneurship, business leadership and education—where and how do these skills and aptitudes affect secondary and higher education?

4. Technology and Media—How do we prepare our students for the rapid onset of this growth?

5. Humanities, Service Organizations and Philosophy—How do we incorporate these into business, education, science, and math in our diversified and global economy?

6. Where and how does history, its people, justice, events and cultures fit into the new paradigm of teaching and learning? How can we incorporate and personalize meaning and relevancy from past occurrences, lives, cultures and philosophies?

7. Medicine—Specializations, Nurturance, Holistic Health and Geriatrics—are we preparing our students for multi-careers and an age of conceptual leadership involving body, mind and spirit?

8. Metaphysics—What can the world of the unseen teach us inside our global diversity, economy and growing population within the context of science, math and education?

What is the meaning of Life?
What is my purpose?
What is reality?
Why am I here?
How did I get here?
Who and What am I?
What will happen when I die?
How can I experience abundance in the areas of health, wealth and happiness?
Who will I be?

If you **knew**, without a doubt in your mind, the answer to each of these questions, would you enjoy every moment of your life? Would you also experience ultimate peace of mind?

9. Positive Psychology—What is happiness, and how does it affect our lives? How does one acquire happiness, and what is its process and relevancy inside schools, businesses and homes?

10. World Peace—Will we get there? What does it look like? How will it affect our national governments? What is the role of gratitude? How do we define the role of the United Nations in this time?

11. Power of Thought, Perspective and Cognitive Behavioral Approaches to Education.

Story-Telling

How would education be affected if retired and veteran educators and parents mentored, meeting regularly with pre-service, new and veteran teachers, sharing their experiences, wisdom and love of children and adolescents? In this new time, *The Fellowship of Sages,* retired and revered educators and parents, did just that. They shared their passions, gifts, stories, challenges and ways of being with students that brought joy and enthusiasm back into the equation of the teaching and learning process. Could there be a greater gift to our students than to call on those educators and parents who chose to participate and contribute inside a child's journey beyond their active teaching years?

What would education look like, and how would students, teachers and parents be positively affected by a Fellowship of Sages? These seasoned educators and parents understood and practiced the power of compassion and service, embedding these components inside all academic subject matter. New teachers were mentored by the Fellowship, entering the classrooms with expanded views and eyes to see beneath the behaviors and words. They brought extensive experiences and a rigorous stance on rich, well-rounded academic growth. But perhaps more importantly, they were privileged in these retirement years to share the expansive perspective of hindsight, educating with an intelligence of mind and heart.

These new teachers were learning to peel back the layers of their students' behaviors, acknowledging the pain, yet observing the innate goodness in all those who walked through their doors. The students provided a means of self-reflection for teachers, and although it was uncomfortable for some, their students' eyes provided an awareness of oneself.

As a novice teacher, Gabe began to understand that taking care of his needs and looking beneath the layers of his students' behaviors wasn't an exact recipe for academic mastery or infallible teaching. He knew there would be horrendous days, making it impossible to think of one positive attribute in that sea of students' faces. Often times, the same held true for his colleagues. And to be accurate, they, the students and co-workers, would sometimes feel the same disdain for him.

Sages and Years Past

The Fellowship of Sages was infiltrated with stories of unrefined interactions between teachers and students, some stories oozing with tears and anger, others flowing into that space where all were learning effortlessly, if even for a day or an hour at a time.

"How may I serve you?" This question was the means of unlocking the closed off and protected hearts of students who "dared you to teach them."

Traditional ways of standardized testing and hours spent in assessment became the conversation for school fodder in 2012. Although heated discussions and disagreements occurred among educators, muddying the intentions and new education policies, changes in assessment continued to pour forth. Dissension and heated emotions shared among colleagues and administration were temporary, providing sharp contrast for what was collectively desired by those teachers and students who were becoming aware and receptive to these changes. The authors at the Arbinger Institute in writing "The Anatomy of Peace" reported, "If we have deep problems, it's because we are failing at the deepest part of the solution. And when we fail at this deepest level, we invite our own failure." [34] The roots of this fragmented system were a hologram of the brokenness and suffering felt by many educators and students.

Assessment

Assessment for the purpose of accountability, student growth and closing achievement gaps would soon die on its own because it simply wasn't working. In years past, standardized tests had overtaken the valuable time teachers and students were expected to cultivate learning and pique curiosity while engaging minds and hearts. The standardized assessments were effective, but not challenging for those students who excelled in math and language.

These were the students who were able to conform to traditional content, or maybe just the students who didn't see any other way to be successful in classrooms. Many of the students were inherently capable of molding their learning profiles and ways of thinking into the rigid assessments, attaining adequate results from standardized and traditional instruction. These students fared well and raised their scores even though they were not enjoying school, as fun and imaginative learning were distant memories from another time. We know of other students, those who resisted the measures, threatening the school's report card each time they attempted to conform—or not!

In recent school history, many urban and charter school teachers with a growing Latino population had spent ten or more weeks a semester evaluating students with various forms of standardized assessments. Assessment preparation became the bulk of most instructional time, creating bored, frustrated and completely disengaged students and teachers. They fared better on many of the tests and made sufficient progress, but critical thinking skills and imaginative design with regard to instruction were small, unattended aspects of numerous teaching curriculums. Teachers had been deeply concerned about the amount of time they spent "teaching to and for the tests" as the cycles of failing schools and disinterested students moved to center stage. Across the nation, the stakes were high and the competition fierce for students who were fortunate to be skilled in mastering the assessment that called for *one solution* and *one way of thought*. These traditional assessments of earlier teaching days left creative problem solving and critical thinking skills partially, if not completely out of the holistic learning and teaching equation.

In 2012, teachers and parents began to envision a world of *educational change* through contrast. Visual Thinking Strategies is a research-based practice that utilizes visual art, assisting students in critical thinking, problem-solving, literacy and communication skills, to name just a few. The Visual Thinking Strategies (VTS) method was created by Abigail Housen, a cognitive psychologist from the Harvard Graduate School of Education. This method became a permanent fixture at Haven Middle School, as the critical components of the visual arts were introduced and explored across many subject areas. Teachers were trained to intimately listen, observe and record the wondrous responses and reflections from students as this research-based strategy was enlisted. The fine arts were generating a renewed interest, with researched-based studies affirming their positive neurological effects on student motivation, while enhancing cognitive skills inside this time of holistic education. In past years, music, physical exercise and thinking strategies that promoted "play" coupled with imagination had been buried beneath policies and mandates that were neglecting the internal wisdom of the very people they were trying to teach and nurture.

With an emphasis on emotional and social learning as core standards, implementing "compassion" into the academic curriculum seemed to be the key unlocking authentic engagement and knowledge. The Fellowship of Sages knew that "serving another" brought the *heart* back into the instructive formula. Curiosity was the new state of mind at Haven Middle School. Educators and parents began to question whether successful management of a system as large as education could be controlled or supervised from the top down. The educational and political leaders of the world began to recognize the positive effects of incremental changes instigated within classrooms, schools and districts. Schools began paying attention to what was going right instead of what was broken and dysfunctional with regard to behaviors, instruction, dialogues and curriculum. This evolution was harrowing, heroic and highly contagious, a systemic transformation that was sweeping in the *new* and ousting the old and dysfunctional. There seemed to be an eternal hope, a malleable vision when invoking a teaching and learning balance of head and heart.

In this time, Gabe and the new teachers were a part of this systemic transformation that began focusing on the power of *perspective*. It was a loaded concept filled with inquiries and affirmative reappraisals of adverse conditions and experiences persons encounter in life. The teachers began to shift their thoughts about the seemingly negative events they were monitoring and mentoring within the schools. They recognized and were aware of the discord and frustrations with time constraints and preparation. They also recognized on some days the outward behaviors of students and teachers felt immensely draining and understatedly wearisome. But perspectives began to shift. Teachers experienced an inner strength, remembering an innate wisdom that consistently appeared when they were called to explore the roots and truths of cause and effect. *"The answers to life's questions reside within."*

Perspectives and Life

There were significant and positive changes in dispositions as teachers at Haven and other urban schools consciously broadened perspectives when negative circumstances and conflicts arose. The Fellowship of Sages met weekly with teachers, where mindful mentoring met with the week's challenges and grievances. Those who practiced the mind exercises of augmenting and shifting perspectives discovered increased optimism and slowly began to enjoy their experiences in and out of the classroom. They observed an unfolding of hope-filled thoughts centering on colleagues, students, and most significantly, themselves. Educators began to deeply understand the power of creative response within their view of the world and its experiences. An *effect* was not a stagnant, isolated and rigid behavior, consequence, or event that sporadically occurred. The teachers remembered that although they could not change an action or the thought of a struggling student, they could affect **how** they responded.

Misunderstandings were explored and defined as *limited perspectives*. When thoughts and feelings are out of alignment, they cause conflict within any family and system, including schools. But as the Sages reminded their students and teachers, schools hold the bright young minds and hearts of children and adolescents learning about life and purpose. Plasticity of thought while serving another led the way to extravagant teaching and learning, recognizing the genius inside every student and educator!

Adolescent Minds

In this new era, teachers were reminded that the age of adolescence is a great and momentous time of brain plasticity. It is a time when potential links and associations between neurons create neural pathways for novel learning and unlimited innovations. When we learn a new skill or think through a problem in a fresh way, we engage various brain cell connections, igniting significant and specific areas in the brain among groups of neuronal connections. Teachers are privileged to be change agents of such an ingenious organic and creative learning process. Martha Kaufeldt, author and educator, explains it this way:

> The human brain is dynamic and constantly re-shaping itself based on its environment and experiences throughout life. This knowledge should influence parents and educators regarding everything they say or do—or don't do—as they contribute to the development of young brains. At the very least, some basic understanding of brain research can not only help teachers realize what teaching methods can maximize learning, but also what methods minimize learning. 35

When we are able to serve another, we begin calling forth the inner wisdom of compassion, activating neural connections in the emotional and cognitive areas of the brain. These neural connections create a firing of neurons that create an outpouring of neuro transmitters like dopamine, which increases positive emotion, enhancing engagement and enthusiasm for learning. The byproduct is that we improve and enrich our minds as well as our students' minds when we engage in optimism and service. Numerous research studies reveal that increased happiness, productivity in work and longevity of life are intimately connected to feelings of compassionate service to another, which increases positive emotion, mental clarity and overall mental and physical health.

"You cannot hate what you do not understand. Other people do not have to change for us to experience peace of Mind and Heart."

International Educational Coalition

Despite numerous disagreements and dissension during this time of national standard planning and selection, the agenda and proposals for national and international school reform programs were taking shape. Countries around the world tended to stay within their cultural comfort zones, but a cohort of educators was established at an international level. International Educational Coalition (IEC) sent members from around the nations and its schools, meeting quarterly to observe the progress of school systems, continually creating and reinforcing relational learning and peace-filled resolutions grounded in *educational and instructional design*.

Students from all over the world were valuable attendees, greatly contributing to each international gathering. There was an authentic desire to begin exploring world peace and its boundaries and limitations. Student led initiatives paved the way for this growing legion of young international participants. The questions asked and the changes explored were constructed and viewed as malleable processes that would continuously require reflection and reinventions for the improvement of the emotional, social and cognitive health of all learners and educators. A service curriculum supported communities of educators in creating and imagining the very best in their students and one another—one student, one classroom and one school at a time.

Power of Stories

Students were encouraged to listen to one another's stories. They listened for cultural values originating from a belief system and thought process that was grounded in tradition, personal ethics and ways of being in a world that was intimately connected to a peer's perspective and personal history. Students were encouraged to acknowledge and cherish the differences and experiences of others. They were asked to literally and figuratively walk in another's shoes as the stories, emotional baggage, and histories of one another were explored and discussed. A self-explanatory style of reaching peaceful resolutions became a powerful intervention for behavioral engagement. This concept or guideline, steeped in observable reverence, was not a blanket rule or immeasurable platitude. The students were actively seeking understanding through-out their school days, discovering ways to demonstrate respect towards one another when disagreements mounted and conflicts spread like viruses.

A Haven of Change

In previous years, Haven Middle School encapsulated an op-pressed and depleted culture filled with robotic and fearful in-structional strategies embedded in the learning and teaching pro-cess. In this new time, middle schools were transforming into places of exploration and experimentation. Gabe and the teams of teachers gathered bi-weekly to discuss challenging real-life, real-time dilemmas. They analyzed the options for resolution on these designated days. Groups of students called on one another and collaborated with a variety of teachers throughout the district (conferencing through Skype), creating an assortment of possible solutions for each quandary presented. The critical thinking and curiosity cited allowed students to often times master twice as many standards in each content area. Traditional assessments con-tinued to inform a number of teaching methodologies, but Indi-vidual Learning Plans continued to expand student intentions, inquiry and a curiosity to know more!

Schools were visited and mentored weekly by physicians, farmers, counselors, business entrepreneurs, nurses, postal work-ers, authors, artists, government workers, finance specialists, ca-reer counselors, retailers, and other professions or skilled employ-ees as all collaborated in working towards relevancy of student learning. Electricians, computer technologists, veterinary assis-tants, hair stylists, clergymen and many other vocations bridged the gaping holes of learning the parts of a sentence and algebraic equations to writing and preparing resumes. This allowed students to discover specific aptitudes for possible intentional goals em-bedded in their Individual Learning Plans and career paths. All who were called to teach and learn sat side by side with the students in creating tasks and projects that brought learning into their homes and futures. *Specialized knowledge* was encouraged in and out of school, as class trips, visiting instructors, and career counselors assisted middle school students with meaning-making and design, invigorating thought processes and meaningful application for future jobs and careers.

Educators joined forces with neuroscientists from around the world as brain development and research-based teaching strategies from the cognitive sciences were explored. The teachers and students were taught how to implement these strategies into most assignments and projects, delving into the conscious and subconscious mind and facets of the brain. Research-based strategies were continually assessed and developed from committees of educators that examined engagement and purposeful principles of cognitive science and positive psychology intertwined with standards and assessments. Teachers learned how positive emotions emit broader perspectives, increasing viable solutions to presented academic and social challenges. Teachers and students remembered and rediscovered how experience changes the physiological structure of the brain when embracing compassion and empathy. (These initial studies were founded in 1964 in labs with rats.)

Positive emotions became the focal points for automatic **reflective processes** and responses inside the brain. How did this occur? Teachers and students studied, researched, and integrated the work of leading experts in the field of mental health and education, who discussed and investigated the intricate relationship of emotion, compassion, and learning.

Teachers and classes were encouraged to implement one action research project each semester, sharing the results with colleagues and parents, showcasing how a comprehensive curriculum and service initiatives muster affirmative change. Teachers and students integrated inquiries into the teaching standards with the assistance, feedback and reflection from parents, teachers, and administrators. The Fellowship of Sages facilitated the action research studies.

Author and psychiatrist Dr. Howard Cutler's notions and thoughts assisted in laying the groundwork of how the role of positive emotion affects individuals and societies. He reiterated, "Studies show that the level of trust in any system directly affects the level of happiness."[36] A level of trust carries specific benefits in overcoming societal problems—trust between groups reduces suspicions, prejudices, discrimination, and conflict. If conflict does happen to arise, trust reduces the likelihood of violence.

Some of the most fascinating and revolutionary findings of this research are the studies showing the potential of positive emotion to transform our exterior world as well as our interior world. In fact, there now appears to be a body of evidence demonstrating that these positive states of mind can directly contribute to not only coping with the world's problems, but actively changing them. New studies have provided experimental evidence that happiness and positive states of mind directly cause people to be more sociable and have more successful social relationships.[37] When we connect with others, there is a greater tendency to open up and share our hearts, forming closer bonds with one another. This was an essential piece of the research because when disagreements or conflicts did occur, those conflicts were lessened because of the shared and discussed social histories.

Educators and students were beginning to trust one another; therefore, the amount of time spent on discipline, behavior management and redirection or re-teaching of subject matter was reduced. Teachers and students were awake, consciously aware and working in sync to form relationships, integrating a deepened respect and trust. This occurred because all were serving one another by acutely listening and therefore summoning a deeper understanding beneath words and behaviors. Respect for one another became a natural outcome of this relational process.

Social Connections and Joy

In this time, the schools began to create a curriculum of *social connectedness*. This plan was not an isolated pull out initiative where students sat, listened, rolled their eyes and then walked or ran to the old patterns of negative behaviors, causing their teachers the tired frustration and repetitive apathy felt by everyone. At Haven Middle School this plan was embedded into the curriculum. (How many character programs across the nation embracing the best of intentions have felt meaningless to students because they were *empty words* that in the students' and teachers' minds were irrelevant and inapplicable?)

In this time of educational evolution, this behavioral plan was applied to real-world interactions. When behavioral and academic issues arose, teachers and students came together, stopped teaching the standard curriculum, and created life *lessons* for all participants in classrooms. By examining the cause, the root of a disallowance of a productive relationship or experiences, all were able to address the intrusive behavior, seldom returning to its toxic cycle of interruption, distraction and negative impacts.

Education began to focus on shared viewpoints, teacher and student commonalities, discovering that when we view one another as human beings with the same desires and goals, conflicts and power struggles begin to disintegrate. Forming broader perspectives, investigating one's thoughts, and serving another became the change agents for renewal and awakening inside class-rooms.

Dr. Martin Seligman, the director of the positive psychology center at the University of Pennsylvania and one of the leading visionaries in this field, proposed that there was more to mental health than just surviving, alleviating the symptoms of mental illness such as depression, anxiety or paranoia.[38] He believed that happiness is grown, and can be cultivated and nurtured to levels of deep satisfaction in life, through our explanatory styles of experiences and events. 39 His notions and words were shared with the students as they examined, argued and challenged his thinking.

What makes us happy? Schools around the nation and world were listening and paying attention to the latest research in these evolving fields of psychology. In prior years, the Fellowship of Sages realized the power of positive emotions and their benefit in forming relationships, affecting physical, emotional and mental clarity. Research had shown that friendship and strong ties to others, inspiring a connectedness, supported happiness. But there was more. Research and empirical studies reported from Dr. Robert Emmons at the University of California, Davis, stated that deep gratitude for life experiences is crucial in broadening perspective and therefore positively affecting physical, mental, emotional and social health.40

Although there were those educational cultures that were still extending school days, emphasizing rigor in math and sciences, and setting higher and higher expectations, many educators began to create expectations that met the student where he or she was, fostering a bond that encouraged the students to excel at a comfortable pace. Educators began teaching about the vital importance of listening to the stories and feelings of those teaching and learning.

The Fellowship of Sages understood that everyone embraces a *personal legend*, one that defines, explains, and eventually carries us to places we never expected. Listening to those stories generated understanding—carving out pathways as one was led to creative revelations and powerful learning. A student's personal legend was written, discussed and re-written as a part of his or her Individualized Learning Plan. *These stories were powerful indicators of the direction of a student's intention.* For example, if a child had argued and fought during class, he or she was asked at a later time to write about how that action helped or hurt his or her learning and behavioral goals, emphasizing the intentional plan.

The prevailing results of deep listening had been discussed by psychologists and counselors for many years. There is a substantial change in a person's thoughts and behaviors just by being listened to, when one is encouraged to hear one's own words and respond to that quiet voice residing within. When we listen, we serve, and when we serve, we become a part of the solution. Adele Faber and Elaine Mazlish, authors of *How to Talk So Kids Will Listen and Listen So Kids Will Talk*, express the importance of attitude in listening and responding for understanding and resolution:

> We can listen with full attention, by acknowledging feelings, and by giving a name to his/her feelings, but more important than any words we use is attitude. If our attitude is not one of compassion, then whatever we say to another will be experienced as phony or manipulative. It is when our words are infused with real empathy that speaks directly to the child's heart. 41

The Fellowship of Sages spoke of gratitude and moving to the heart. They understood that when the heart is open, the mind follows, paying attention and synthesizing subject matter. Academic mastery triumphs every time.

Envisioning

At Haven Middle School, each person remembered to focus on the *essence* of every student, colleague, administrator and parent who appeared to be behaving poorly. When one's focus shifted to seeing the innate goodness of all persons, a positive change occurred in the behaviors and words of the one who was struggling.

Literally, Gabe could see and feel the effects of what he desired and envisioned from his students when he and others practiced this visualizing process with compassion and fortitude. These shifts began to trickle into one heart, one classroom, and one school after another. These envisioning subtleties were incremental but significantly felt from the bottom up and from inside out. *What we envision becomes the reality with a little time and patience.*

Gabe spent the first several weeks of school gathering information about his students' interests, motivations, strengths and what troubled or challenged them. He learned of their academic readiness levels and where he needed to begin. He learned of their passions and what their behaviors truly indicated when he stepped back—only observing. Together, he and the students created graphs, tables and journals that demonstrated where each was performing while understanding academic content and how it transferred to worldly knowledge on a daily basis. Mastery of content was just a part of the puzzle. Educators dove inside student intentions and life goals, creating relevancy in any and every teaching standard they could find. Together teachers, parents and students created, reflected and re-created Individualized Learning Plans.

Self and group assessments were significant teaching tools in the secondary schools. Gabe and his team of teachers began to assess and plan for each student's future with incremental steps. The emphasis of these plans was not directed towards the end product, but focused on the daily process of each student. Initially this felt time-consuming and arduous, but as weeks and months passed, Gabe and the teams of teachers flew through standards, wrapping up the objectives one by one across the curriculum. Gabe observed his students explore, master, then artfully build on their strengths, applying the knowledge to outside projects and assignments. Although there were moments when any other career but teaching felt appealing, Gabe felt the excitement more often than the frustration. This was enough to keep going!

There were "personal days" termed *heart health days* built into the school year for students and teachers, taking the time they needed to rest and renew. Absences and tardiness dropped significantly as the students were given time in and out of class to power down and rejuvenate, even for a five-minute break for crackers and a drink of water. *Crackers and a drink of water*—this was enough to curb absences in the first semester by over 20%! Test scores skyrocketed because **everyone** was teaching and learning. Physicians, counselors, community business leaders, psychologists, parents and students asked the questions that were relevant to the presented standards. Retired teachers, many of whom were Sages in the Fellowship, returned to the schools to share their wisdom. Both students and former teachers benefitted from these experienced and wise educators who taught from a place where novel methods and innovative technologies could not reach.

Celebrations and Chaos in a Middle School Classroom

Tamara, an outspoken and ardent young woman in the eighth grade who seemed to carry a chip on her shoulder if someone looked at her for a second longer than she perceived appropriate, battled Gabe every morning during the first half of the second semester. She refused assignments, shot caustic comments across the room, smacked her lips in disgust, never turned in an assignment, and threatened her perceived adversaries with words and fists. Others seemed to follow her lead, disrupting and blaming each other for every perceived insult or comment. One utterance or perceived expression would send the class and grade level into complete chaos and turmoil.

Driving to school one morning, Gabe felt the urge to pass the den of recent frustration and grief. "Hell, they don't pay me enough to put up with this shit day after day. Talking to myself again… Jesus!" Lately, Gabe had felt like a failure when it came to teaching Tamara, and truthfully, many of the other students. Sighing, he hesitantly pulled into the parking lot as the old Explorer seemed to coerce him to its temporary home, the corner space where it occupied a nine-hour position five or six days a week.

This morning despair signaled its return emitting a dull ache between Gabe's shoulder blades. A group of students, rumored to have joined another recent gang, were throwing nasty and inappropriate comments, bullying each other with no intention of settling down to learn. Pulling up his tall "teaching" stool, Gabe just sat and observed the crowd of raucous bodies. He thought about nothing and just observed, falling into a trance where the only thought that entered his mind was one of escape. The background laughter and chatter seemed to drop away as emptiness swallowed up everything around him.

A couple of the students noticed Gabe sitting and staring at them. Turning towards Gabe, they hesitated and then asked, "Hey, Mr. G, what's up? You look weird. What's wrong with you?" Other students were curious now as the bells had rung and yet the classroom was void of leadership and guidance. "Mr. G, say something." Now most of the class was attentive to the oddity of Gabe's demeanor. He turned to look out the window, and his heart picked up a beat. He thought of Mr. Eden, the Fellowship, the notebooks, and the holes in his life in the time when weed and alcohol were his best friends; and then he remembered *this place.*

Stories have the power to heal...

Gabe turned to the class. "It looks as if no one is in the mood to work on expository writing, so I am going to tell you a story." Incredibly, the class remained quiet as Gabe held their attention for at least another 30 seconds.

"I have acted like an ass most of my life." There were several quiet chuckles, but Gabe smiled and continued. "I had to learn the hard way until I found this wild and strange treasure... about 12 years ago."

"What are you talking about Mr. G.?"

"What treasure, and what did you do that was so bad?" students shouted out, laughing.

Gabe walked over to his desk and opened a drawer. The old wooden box with the bent rusted latch appeared behind some stacks of envelopes and notebook paper. Lifting the old box from the drawer, he carried it to his stool and sat down, holding it carefully. "This," he said, holding up the box, "changed my life, and I don't know if you will relate or understand, but I feel it's time to share a little about myself and this old box."

The students were quiet. It was an uncomfortable quiet, not knowing what to expect from the leader of their class, as a few sneered quiet comments, others shushed them, and most of the students just sat cautiously, waiting for Gabe's direction. Tamara's head was on her desk, outwardly excluding the room and its tenuous and questionable atmosphere.

"The choices I made at about 14 years old were not so great." Gabe took a long breath and stared at the box. "One day my dad just up and died. I hated the world. I couldn't imagine a world without him, so I fought everyone and everything." Looking down at the box, Gabe felt that familiar lump in his throat, but he pushed on. "I fought with my fists, my words, but mostly my thoughts. I forgot how to be even a little bit happy, but mostly I forgot how to trust. I didn't give a damn about anyone. No one, and I mean no one, felt sorrier for me than me, so I tried to numb myself out, but feeling hopeless just became a part of my life. And truthfully, I became addicted to those depressing thoughts. I hated school and was failing most of my classes, and what was worse, my mom needed me, but I couldn't stand to be home and to see her so sad. She was hurting too, but I didn't care, or thought I didn't care."

Gabe felt the familiar burning and swelling of his eyes. He pinched the bridge of his nose to keep the tears from washing him away. *Jesus, what the hell am I doing?* he thought for a moment.

The students didn't move or speak, and the only sound heard was the fan buzzing in the back of the room. It eloquently provided the background music for a story that had to be remembered and shared, because the story was not just Gabe's, it was a story for many. Gabe looked out at the faces of those he had promised to teach, those he had promised to serve, and those who were teaching him in every moment. Stepping off the stool, he moved to an empty chair and sat with a group of students at the corner table.

"After joining a gang, endless drinking and almost overdosing on a few occasions, I ended up in a rehab center, where my life took off in a different direction."

The classroom was a tomb of silent anticipation.

"So… one night I had a dream, or more like a nightmare at the time."

Several students interrupted, "What happened, Mr. G.? Tell us!"

The students seemed to sense Gabe's hesitation in relating the story. Turning around, Gabe looked down. Tamara's head and arms were lifelessly sprawled across the table with her backpack still attached to her shoulders. Gabe could see her eyes fluttering, and her tear stained cheeks were luminescent from the glare of the floor lamp sitting next to her.

"I gave in. I just quit fighting because I wanted something more, something different. Somehow in *this place*, inside the dream, I remembered who I really was, with the help of my grand-father." Gabe felt it was more than a dream, but he could never explain this to his students, and did it really matter? "I do remember crying a lot in the dream, and even during the times when I remembered it weeks or months later, I cried. It was so strange… I felt like I was kind of dying, but I didn't want to die and not live anymore, I just wanted to die to all the ways I had caused myself to suffer and those around me."

Gabe stood up and moved to another table sitting in the corner. "It was surreal… when I opened this box, there was a piece of clay, and somehow when I held it in my hands and looked at it, I saw all the life I hadn't lived yet and some experiences of my past." The room was starting to rumble with whispers as chairs tilted on their back legs—squeaking, announcing some discomfort and agitation from these words and from a man who was speaking of strange events. These were not the usual words of lessons, discussions or presentations. There were more quiet whispers and uncomfortable laughter.

"Where'd the box come from? I thought you dreamed this?" Tamara shouted out, staring directly into Gabe's eyes.

"I still don't understand what really happened, Tamara, and I don't know where the box came from, but after that dream or whatever it was, my life slowly began to change in how I saw myself and the world. After the dream, for a few years, I still acted like a jerk and didn't follow so many rules... or for that matter the laws too well, but there was something different. Something had changed. I just somehow knew I was going to be okay and I could do anything I wanted with my life."

"How much money you make, Mr. G, and look at where you are?"

More laughter and cajoling with this last comment, but Gabe smiled. "I make enough, and I love what I do... so far." He grinned at the group in the back. "I'm not saying every day is perfect or I'm always happy and singing in the shower, but there is lots to do in the world, and you've got a buffet of choices out there, guys." Gabe smiled and stood up. He walked through the rows of tables and touched the shoulders of each student. "I can't tell you what to do or how to do it, and I can't save you from your own decisions or choices, but I can be there for you and listen. I can be there when your days are lousy and lonely and your heart feels as if it is being shattered, and the lump in your throat feels bigger than a damn basketball."

Gabe picked up the old wooden box and held it in his hands. "You all have this box, a treasure you can open and look into anytime you want." Gabe placed his large, calloused hand over the center of his chest and returned to his stool in the front of the classroom.

"You've got to listen to this." He patted his chest and looked around the room. "It is the only teacher that will steer you in the direction of your dreams."

Gabe walked over to Tamara and laid the old wooden box on the table beside her. "I don't need it back, and you can share it with someone else someday if you choose to." Tamara looked at the box and touched it with a couple of fingers and then pushed it aside. Gabe remembered shoving the box out of his sight and thinking it was bullshit, but time would be on Tamara's side, just like it had been for him. He understood this well.

The class began to chatter, and uncomfortable laughter followed as the students continued to monitor this strange behavior and the odd words from their teacher. Gabe walked around the tables and gathered up the papers the students had started less than a half hour ago.

"Hey, Mr. G., are we done with class today? Why are you picking up our papers?"

Gabe looked over in the direction of the questions. "We are changing directions." Picking up his cell, he slid his fingers over a few letters and numbers. The text was sent.

Appreciation

After collecting the partially completed assignment of outlines and mind maps, Gabe pulled out the journals and began passing them around the room. "You can begin to write out your thoughts or any feelings you have about the day or our conversation or anything that comes to mind, but when we return to the classroom, I want you to note or draw of three experiences or people you feel grateful for. I believe we may be taking an *experience trip*, so gather your jackets and IDs and prepare to leave in the next 15 minutes."

Gabe switched on the iPod as Mozart's *Serenade No. 13 for Strings* filtered through the classroom. The students, wondering and contemplating what was next, took out their pens and began writing, drawing and discussing the strange morning events with one another. The preparations for spontaneous *experience trips* had been planned as part of the curriculum during the summer months and weeks leading up to the beginning of the school year. Because Haven was collaborating with community professionals in and out of the classroom, the curriculum, students, parents and teachers had planned for spur-of-the-moment teaching episodes that would often times take place outside the walls of school.

Within a few minutes, Gabe's phone vibrated with the response he had hoped for. The students were preparing to serve and to be served in the next hour. Gabe and his class piled into a bus with a guidance counselor, two members of the Fellowship and three high school students. They arrived on the pediatric oncology/hematology unit within minutes and resumed their learning and teaching.

Common Humanity

The classroom on the oncology unit was filled with children and adolescents who were experiencing challenges with their physical health and desired to maintain a lifestyle that felt as normal as possible considering their consummate medical and health needs and challenges. These children and adolescents on the unit also experienced the frustrations with fulfilling their social and emotional needs as their hearts beat with an overwhelming desire for normalcy, health, friendships, outings, and freedom from worry about dying. They desired an improved way of *being and feeling* within this medicinal environment. Some days, it was difficult not to be eaten up with fear of the unknown, but when Haven students showed up, their fears lessened and even diminished for a few hours. When one observed the desires and needs of all the children and adolescents, both oncology patients and students from Haven, one noticed a collective presence of acceptance and even a little joy in just coming together.

Compassion was modeled at Haven Middle School by focusing and giving attention to the students' *commonalities*. They were encouraged to discover their common traits rather than their distinct differences, which typically took on the thought form of an "in group" versus "out group" mentality or "us against them or me against you." The students gradually became aware of their shared purposes and goals through the discussion of their stories that spoke of similarities rather than differences.

This was part of the new curriculum in 2012. Commonality between students and staff was integrated into many of the experience trips so that students could begin thinking about their connections with one another. It transcended the teaching and learning process within the walls of a school, reaching out into the world where a burning desire to live peacefully with one another was discussed and explored. On that winter morning inside the hospital, there was not a single student, patient, doctor, nurse, counselor or teacher standing in the commons area that did not hope for improvement in their lives and for those around them.

Gabe's class washed up, put on their protective clothing, and proceeded to create a very different learning opportunity as they began sharing books and stories, communicating in primitive ways; ways that did not require formal conversation or the formalities and personas persons don when trying to impress or give off an air of superiority. There seemed to be a profound understanding between students and patients as each spoke with gestures, expressions, but mostly with a primordial understanding of one another's feelings. The laughter was contagious as a few of the physicians who had visited and taught at Haven lingered in the hospital classroom joining in on the levity. Algebra problems were attempted, literature genres discussed, and the steps to scientific experiments explored. All worked together for a common solution—*to feel better.*

Dr. Martin Seligman from the University of Pennsylvania in his research and studies knows the power of turbo charging joy. He says, "To make a gratitude visit, writing a letter or sharing your gratitude with someone just once shows measurably happier and less depressed persons a month later." Less powerful but more lasting is an exercise he calls three blessings, taking time each day to write down a trio of things that went well and why. People are less depressed and happier three months later and six months later. 42

Gabe and the class returned to Haven later that morning. The students resumed their journal writing of gratitude and revised their intentions. On mornings like this one, students had no trouble focusing on one another's commonalities. There were no in-groups and out-groups as they wrote of people as people and not of people as objects.

The students' feelings and thoughts belonged to every child and adolescent inside and outside the walls of Haven Middle School. The trip to the oncology unit was not one of grandeur or showcasing a school on the rise of progressive learning. It was part of a life curriculum, and it began creating a *unity of hearts*. The arguments, harsh words and bullying of one another had been distracted and interrupted by a remembrance of human compassion and commonality. There was not a more effective lesson or curriculum for adolescents searching for meaning in life. The students struggling with behavioral issues, family matters and poverty of all kinds were united with those children and adolescents who were presented with physiological and emotional challenges. Both patients and students were simply children that morning, coming together to share, and in all honesty, *to feel better.*

Teachings from the Fellowship of Sages

The Fellowship of Sages understood well that when we begin to serve another, we paradoxically reach within—discovering the joy and peace that is our innate birthright. The children gathered on the oncology unit's class-room were subconsciously or consciously planting the seeds of *inner strength* and a life curriculum that transported them outside the walls of sickness, medicinal procedures, curriculum, and standardized testing. The age of accountability called out and the answers bellowed inside their hearts, the only place that mattered. The paradox was alive and vibrant as *perspective* was remembered, for it is the engine that drives all persons to well-being and hearts towards peace.

The world of education was slow to change, but the progression was active and expansive in many minds and hearts of students and teachers deeply listening to the feelings and thoughts of one another. There were still many people who believed that serving another was an act of giving away, a spiritual gesture, a Sunday or holiday activity isolated from daily living. Those notions could not have been farther from the truth, as educators around the world began to feel the power and magic of its effects. They began to understand how compassion breeds personal happiness and a sense of pleasure in one's life. The notion of integrating compassion into the center of the academic curriculum was a slowly expanding movement, but *hope* lead the way, tugging at the minds and hearts of those teaching and learning.

School Days

There were rough days and moments when much of the time in class seemed to circle and spin in caustic comments, frustration and aggravated behaviors, but it didn't last for long. A journey was emerging where students, parents, and teachers began to go within, instead of looking for advice off the pages of books or in the ego directives of another. The Sages had taught of an individual process... a journey in which one is aware of whom he or she is that teaches while listening to the intelligence of the heart.

Parker Palmer, teacher and author of The Courage to Teach, *eloquently stated,*

> *I am a teacher at heart, and there are moments in the classroom when I can hardly hold the joy. But at other moments, the classroom is so lifeless or painful or confused— and I am so powerless to do anything about it, that my claim to be a teacher seems a transparent sham. Then the enemy is everywhere: in those students from some alien planet, in the subject I thought I knew, and in the personal pathology that keeps me earning my living this way.* 43

We serve another as we begin with ourselves, taking an authentic look inside our minds and hearts. (Fellowship of Sages, 2012)

This exploration happened in late February of Gabe's first year at Haven. Haven and other schools were flourishing in many ways. There was a sense of an expanding community that could not be described or denied. An unspoken attitude of *respect* for another permeated the halls and classrooms even when disagreements and conflicts escalated, threatening to rip apart the very fragile newly constructed foundation that was beginning to pulsate throughout the schools and lives of those who were teaching and learning. Haven Middle School was felt to be a safe place to argue, disagree or converse in ways that challenged the thinking of each administrator, teacher, parent and student. It was not a utopian environment bereft of fiery emotions and days filled with egos and platitudes washed in sarcasm or hopelessness—there were plenty. But there was a *recovery process*, a collective resiliency that took hold when dialogues resumed and awareness of heart intelligence was remembered and implemented.

Tamara did not return to school for several days following the trip to the pediatric oncology unit. Gabe called the two numbers listed on her emergency forms, but there was no response. She lived with her father and his girlfriend, and after six days, a withdrawal notice arrived. When Catherine shared the news with

Gabe, he started thinking the worst, but then stopped. Hell, he had no idea what Tamara's daily life was like, and maybe she was off to a better place.

Following dismissal, after receiving the withdrawal notice, Gabe excused himself from a research study group. Irritated, he drove the Ford Explorer through the narrow neighborhood streets into an area that reeked of poverty. A small adobe house surrounded by a few cacti and a gravel drive matched the numbers on the emergency form. The tiny dilapidated dwelling stood somberly, greeting Gabe with a torn punched-in screen of what used to be a front door. Gabe knocked a few times, noticing a couple plastic and grimy animal bowls filled with bits of debris and a splash of rusty water. Gabe's hollow knock was answered with a few faint meows from inside the house, but nothing more. He waited a few more minutes, knocking sporadically, then reluctantly trudged to his car.

Driving back along the narrow streets, his mind wandered to *that place*—the place where his sadness and gloom had been intensified, then released. Did Tamara have the wooden box he had handed her that morning? She had disappeared for now, but her presence hung heavy in Gabe's heart. Where the hell was she? Why did it matter so much? he wondered as he pulled into the gym. Playing basketball might give his mind a break from the lamenting thoughts that had plagued him all afternoon, but there was something else… a stinging remembrance he couldn't quite name. He let it go and played ball.

Restless Night

The pub seemed louder and smokier than usual as he swirled the beer around in his mug. He pulled out his phone and scrolled to Catherine's number, but then decided otherwise. Placing it in his back pocket, he announced his departure. "I'm out of here," he said, throwing a few bucks on the table.

"What's your hurry? The game hasn't even started." Joel laughed, glancing up at Gabe, and then looked concerned.

Shrugging his shoulders, Gabe patted Joel on the top of his head. "Got some things to take care of, and hey, don't forget to collect my winnings!" Gabe grinned and hurried out, pushing through the crowds, noise, and stench of stale liquor and memories...

The *things* Gabe needed to take care of were closer to him than he wished as his head swam with thoughts and his insides tugged at his chest with feelings he could not name. Pulling into his apartment, he felt exhausted from the day. Why? He just couldn't keep his attention on much of anything... distraction was imminent. The hot shower helped. He stood under the new shower heads and allowed the steaming water to wash away the accumulated feelings of hopelessness he had begun to dredge up with many of his students and their lives... and now Tamara had just disappeared.

Gabe was too tired to begin any schoolwork tonight. Lying on the couch, he flipped through a couple of channels, hesitating when he found the ball game, but his mind was elsewhere. He opened the sliding glass door and fell back on the couch, feeling the cool breezes sweep into the room, lulling him into a fairly rapid and deep sleep.

Dream

Gabe stood in the center of a large empty gymnasium bouncing a basketball as the huge metal doors clicked and then methodically opened. Mr. Eden walked in. His grandfather grinned as he walked over to Gabe, holding out his hand and patting his chest with the other hand. Gabe turned and quickly walked over to the man he loved, noticing a bright glowing glob flickering in Mr. Eden's palm.

"Look at you, Gabe my boy. You have saved a life. Don't quit now, the journey is just getting started." Mr. Eden grinned, handing the glob of clay to Gabe.

Looking down, he tossed the basketball towards the bleachers and felt the warmth of the clay fill his entire body. "You were there… in that place… weren't you?"

Gabe looked up as Mr. Eden nodded his head. "You've got to start trusting your gut, Gabe. It hasn't let you down yet."

"What do you want me to do, and what the hell do you mean?" The clay grew brighter as Gabe observed the vivid colors, and then chills began to filter their way through his entire body. He just stood there shaking, teeth chattering, and for a moment, he felt the familiar embrace of his grandfather's arm linked tightly around his shoulder.

Opening his eyes, Gabe's teeth were still slightly chattering as he turned over on the old couch. The tattered afghan was twisted around his boxers, and he frantically kicked it off, jerking upright. The former breeze had turned into heavy gusts as the wind chimes were ringing like mighty cathedral bells while the blinds knocked into the panes on the sliding glass door. His gaze moved around the living room. "Mr. Eden," he whispered, "whose life is saved?" The room was silent.

"GRANDFATHER, where the hell are you? Jesus, you can't just appear and then nothing!" Gabe stood up and paced the living room. He slammed the sliding glass door shut, noticing his phone lying on the coffee table right where he had left it. "Shit, I'm talking to myself and a dead man." Putting his hands on the sides of his head, he fell back down on the couch, leaned forward and closed his eyes. "Breathe, Gabe, just breathe."

Suddenly a pang, sort of a spasm accompanied with a dull ache, darted through his chest, *a chest pain…* but this time, he wasn't worried. Looking up, he excitedly grabbed his chest and laughed out loud. This was it—the pain in his chest was a message

... a word from the wise—from a teacher who exemplified greatness because he was always the student.

Gabe shook his head and patted the center of his chest. "You've got to listen to this... it hasn't let you down yet." A life had been saved—his own.

"It's all good, Grandfather. It's all damn good."

New Day

A slice of the sun lingered and then peeked behind a few clouds through the morning mist. It felt as if the partial wedge of sun was breathing in and out, ridding itself of the dark night as the swirls and bands of turquoise and pink prepared entry for the majestic yellow. Gabe walked over to the door and stretched. His body ached from the lumps and bumps of a well-worn 40-year-old couch. Walking into the kitchen, desperate for caffeine, he stopped, noticing three hummingbirds at the feeder collecting their nourishment for a day in the mountains...

"In any crisis there is always hope and improvement in the places that feel broken and non-functional, if, one has the eyes to see." His grandfather's voice rang out in the quiet kitchen.

The days and weeks of the spring semester passed with a lot of activity. There were notions and fresh ideas. Yet, beneath the activity of an inner city middle school, there was hope, and that is all Gabe could give his colleagues and students. Truth be told, that was all he could give to Tamara so many months ago. It was enough.

He focused on all that was going well. He took care of himself, therefore creating plenty of mind and heart to share with his students. He remembered that the *only life one can save is one's own.* He kept in mind that the imagination and creative visions of well-being held his new stories brimming with desire and possibility. When he forgot, a mild but significant chest pain would always remind him. For that, he was grateful.

Epilogue

Winter 2011

Maybe teacher effectiveness highlighting student growth should be measured with Individual Learning Plans developed by educators, students, and parents, demonstrating the intentions, projects, assessments, discussions and student performance incurred through a school year? If these assessment measures sound impossible, I think we could all use some minor chest pains these days. We will need to experience some discomfort, angst, and confusion as we create a compassionate presence inside our schools, homes and businesses. It is not impossible; it will just take some time, patience, and a collaborative effort to shift perspective and recreate what we know is not working and what we know to be true.

The national media still continues to project and compete for the "bad news," or the curious fates of superstar athletes and performers, the homicides, suicides and the slow, degrading illusion of an economy gone awry. National healthcare, education policies, and the ongoing world conflicts are tossed around as we hear about the troves of political dissension, job loss, and a national educational system that is vulnerable while attaining progress, yet lamenting over end results.

There is no doubt that as a culture, we are drawn to the drama of experiences and events that create fear, a skewed excitement, and unrest in our minds. But somehow, there seems to be a shift, a change in thoughts and feelings as many educators, parents and students are beginning to choose a different perspective, one that is catching the attention of the teaching and learning process, building relationships one student, one class, and one school at a time. Compassion seems to be present, but sometimes buried in the debris of drama, injurious competition and old thought patterns.

"Let me know how I may serve you in the days and weeks to come." Mr. Pickett understood perspective and possibility. He placed his eyes on what he desired to see.

"Take me to the place you cry from, where the storm blows your way." This lyric is taken from a song, "Inside Your Heaven," sung by Carrie Underwood. When we step inside our students,' parents,' or our colleagues' worlds, looking deeper than the spewed words and outward behaviors, we serve one another in imaginative ways; ways that enable us to find our inner treasure, our heart that never lets us down when we get quiet and listen.

As state educational budgets continue to undergo revenue reductions and spending cuts, with possibly more to come, prioritization will become an important issue. I hope I am wrong, but education might take further financial hits, depending upon each individual state. So what does prioritizing look like in the face of these economic and accountability dilemmas and times?

It begins with a different stream of thinking. What am I without dreams and a creative vision of what I desire for education in the future? What are you without dreaming and desiring something different for yourself and the world around you? These questions were the impetus for this book, and although many might disagree, telling me it is a lollipop world in which I live to write of such changes in education, I know differently. I know that there were no sewing machines, computers, telephones, Disney Worlds, digital movies and life as we know it without creative visions, all manifesting once we placed our thoughts with a desire and deep belief in the possible.

We have become a culture of quick fixes. When depressed we take a pill; when we need to lose weight, we go on a temporary diet with an all-or-nothing mentality in place. When we desire to build muscle, we ingest products that hopefully will do this for us, and when something feels broken or out of balance, we frantically search for solutions, techniques and strategies to improve the perceived problems. When laws are broken and rules are not followed, we tighten the reins and punish, lashing out and often times finding ourselves in a deeper, bleaker hole—one that feels impossible to ascend.

We have forgotten that everything we are and see was initially experienced in the *mind* before it became our reality. How we feel and the thoughts we hold positively or negatively affect us, creating circumstance, experience and relationships within and around us. It is as author and motivational leader Napoleon Hill taught of long ago: knowledge is not power—it is mindful intention, burning desires and positive thinking of oneself and those around one that foster abundance in all areas of life.

As a society, we have been conditioned to believe we must know the answers to problems or presented challenges, and if we do not, it is a sign of unintelligence or weakness. Yet when we embrace the courage to ask the questions, challenging old stories and traditions we have been conditioned to believe are right and just, we open our minds and perspectives to novel ways of seeing the world. We keep our focus and attention on what is going well and what is in our control. We listen to the heart intelligence, the resiliency of the heart beating the rhythmic truths of each person. This requires us to take deep breaths in the moment of acute stress, visualizing a happier, more peaceful moment when our worlds appeared brighter and calm. If we cannot recall an experience to visualize, then we imagine for a minute or two breathing back into the center of our chests, where the electromagnetic and healing powers of the heart reign supreme.

Our students are calling out to us through boredom, defiance, truancy, and failing test scores. Beneath the layer of insubordination and apathy is a distinct desire and voice that yearns to question the status quo, longing for improvement in relationships and experiences, but most importantly, improvement in how one *feels*.

This is anything BUT a selfish notion, and one that promulgates empathy. Dr. Howard Cutler states, "Since compassion involves the ability to sense another's suffering, one must have at least some degree of empathy for the other person."[44]

There is an impressive body of research gathered over the last two decades that consistently demonstrates practicing empathy will reduce the emotional and perceived gap of differences between us and others. We are innately and infinitely connected to one another; as social beings, we are completely capable of feeling the joy and suffering of another. When we empathize, we empower our minds with an ability to deeply feel the emotions of others. When we reach out based on those emitted emotions, we not only serve others, we serve ourselves, gleaning personal happiness with a proclivity for social and global happiness. Why not? Can you think of a better dream to collectively envision or create? Is there a better curriculum to embed inside instruction for our students and children, our future world citizens?

How may I serve you? What do you need? How can I assist you? I understand. I am so sorry. What would make this easier for you? What do you think we should do? How are you feeling? Often times, solutions are discovered by being heard. We do not always require another's opinion or judgment. It is enough to be heard and to hear ourselves retell the story. Somewhere deep down in the telling of that story is an inner teacher, the heart that is ready and available to share its wisdom.

Our intuition is a muscle of the imagination. It seems to have lost much of its power and significance in these times of teaching and learning as we try to support one another in our volitions of academic success. Implementing and trusting the intuitive process takes practice and time and carries an immense value inside academic curriculum, relationships and life, removing us from states of limbo and confusion into places of clarity and pleasure. Using the gift of intuition is worth the effort and practice.

To think an author is an expert in the content of what he or she writes is a grave mistake, and one that flows with the premise "we teach what we need to learn." What piques my curiosity and urges my notions into action is *what I do not fully understand or struggle to know*. Writing this book has assisted in the process of examining my own life, the beliefs (bundles of thoughts) I nurture and the ways I communicate with others. My journey is just beginning as I traverse through contrast, selecting what I prefer to experience in each moment, consciously or subconsciously. With joyful anticipation I look forward to the adventurous journey alongside my students, children and colleagues, listening deeply for ways to serve.

How May I Serve You? is a story of paradox. To actively serve another is to silently listen and be with another. When we listen, we steer our students and colleagues toward the guidance of the heart, the intelligence that transcends the biological constraints of the three-pound organ, the brain. In this act of compassionate guidance lies the gentle awakening of our life's questions and quandaries waiting exploration through renewed perspectives. Yet, we need the brain as an instrument to intuit the knowledge and content we uncover when we feel affirmed, safe and invigorated in creating new solutions.

When we ask the question of service, our minds and hearts desire to be in alignment with an attitude of compassion. We in turn feel open for a novel response, one we might not have thought about when communicating from a place of angst and narrowed thinking, eliminating our ability to completely understand one another.

The question *How may I serve you?* is contained in the old wooden box with the rusted latch, the container of our dreams, the matrix of all that we are and are becoming. Are we the potters in our lives, embracing limitless possibilities much grander than what is seen with the eyes and experienced through the other senses?

The thoughts we create, either through abundance or poverty, show up in almost every aspect of our lives. What do you choose to see? Grab what grabs you... Be patient with the chaos of change, as this is the essential element of the creative process, but become excited about the opportunities inside every mind and heart. The only limitations are those we impose upon ourselves and our thinking. *How may I serve you?* It is the question of educational evolution, and one we are ready to ask...

"There is no use in trying," said Alice; "One can't believe impossible things."

"I dare say you haven't had much practice," said the Queen. "When I was your age, I always did it for half an hour a day. Why, sometimes I've believed as many as six impossible things before breakfast."

~ Lewis Carroll

It was once written:

And the day came when the risk to remain tight in a bud was more painful than the risk it took to blossom.

~ Anais Nin

Reflections from First Year Teachers
from Indianapolis Teaching Fellows
(The New Teacher Project)

I have collected several reflections from first-year teachers created in my graduate classes at Marian University. I have discovered a common ground when these new teachers are desiring to see improvement in academic mastery. That commonality is voiced in building relationships with their students while creating a foundation grounded in heart intelligence and therefore excellence in cognitive retention and retrieval.

Teacher Reflection One

Overall, I have developed great relationships with all of my students. Many students tell me that they only do work in my class because they like my class and I teach things differently than their other teachers. I honestly don't know what it is I am doing that the students appreciate, but I just plan on continuing teaching the way I am. I treat my students with respect, I talk to them when I see them in the hallways, I joke around with them, and I encourage their work. I feel that by doing all of that, my students respect me and my class and work hard to do well; and while doing so, they are closing the achievement gap that may be present in science.

Teacher Reflection Two

In order to make my class as interesting as possible to keep the students' attention, I try to mix things up and do things in class that I enjoy doing too, whether it is projects, games, or other activities. At times, yes, we do have to take notes, but overall, I try to limit the amount of reading and note-taking my students do.

Bringing in college course work is a great idea! I keep telling them that college is all notes and studying, but I don't think they get it. I would love to bring in my old notebooks, but they are all in Germany! :)

I've built some incredible relationships with some of my students. It seems like the more difficult ones are really attracted to me. I am a "discipline kid" magnet! I wouldn't say I treat them any differently, and maybe that is why they reach out to me. I don't see them as "problem students" and I make sure to always treat them with respect. You will often hear me correct someone's behavior with something silly or a quick role reversal or a crazy accent or with the question "How do you think you could re-phrase that and actually get what you want?" So many of my students just want to be heard and seen and valued. I understand this because I find all of them really interesting. However, I feel like I should be capitalizing on that advantage more.

One more thing, I think: always be human—not super teacher, not always perfect. I readily admit when I am wrong, have made a mistake or been unfair. I also act like a complete fool on a regular basis! Laughter is important!

I think that anything that is required of you that scares you to bits or makes you feel really out of your element is exactly what you need. It is in those moments of feeling completely "other" that we connect in a real way with each other and find deep wells of empathy and compassion. Sending college kids to help build schools in Africa or teach street kids how to read and speak English in India or to debate the merits of democracy in European seminars is exactly what they need. We can be so spoiled and insular and the perspective that you gain from the vantage point of a different country is priceless. Sorry, on my soap box again!!

I agree with Nichole—I think it would be a fantastic idea for seniors to have to do some sort of service project/hours as part of their graduation requirement. I think stepping outside of your own "bubble" (even when it's a really nice bubble, but especially if it's a tough one), and learning to see the world from someone else's perspective is invaluable to students (and adults!). I think this type of exposure would really help them on an emotional/ maturity level in entering college.

Teacher Reflection Three

Although I do not teach high school, I would imagine that one way to engage the students in my math lessons would be to contact all the connections I made in college, the folks in the math department (and other depts.) at IU, to get guest speakers or arrange a visit to Bloomington to see the campus. It is true that not all students will go to college, and this is not meant to contradict a reply to a previous post, but maybe those students who are not going to college just think that they cannot afford it, or have never been to a campus. I am sure that there are students that are on the fence and can afford to leave home, who are also worth fighting for. That is, I have students who are not the "Precious" of the family, but who are scraping by, like Mom, my siblings, and me did through the 80s and 90s, and these students, once they see a campus and realize that good grades can pay for school, can help swing the stats on who goes and stays in college.

For those students who are not planning to attend college, there are other places a class could travel to see how math (or whatever your subject) relates to the real world; and that's really the point, isn't it? Of course a great majority of us have classrooms that consist of students who we may not want to take out into a public setting; for fear that their behavior will be too embarrassing, or worse... I would refer those of us with classroom management to Robert's post above about building relationships with our students. Proactive approaches to issues have worked (at a middle school level on 10th St.) and I think that I would take my students just about anywhere (with chaperones). Motivating our kids requires us to show them their options after "this," whatever "this" may be.

Teacher Reflection Four
(Response to a Power Point)

Slide 23 asks "What are the four basic understandings that encourage pro-social behaviors and how do they look in a classroom?" I think we all strive to teach the true meaning of respect to our students. It is such a big issue with 7th graders! I found out very quickly that my students talked extensively about being disrespected, but couldn't really put into words what respect really is. We role played what respect looks like and what disrespect looks like, but getting it into words was really difficult—even for me! In the end, we felt that respect was individual and that a lot of times it isn't about what it said but how it is said. Tone is everything. We also talked about how we can communicate our respect in ways that are obvious so that miscommunication doesn't happen. I often model the behavior I expect to see in my class by asking if something was meant disrespectfully or if I'm just being overly sensitive. Students recognize that they do behave in ways that are disrespectful and often because they are processing some other slight from earlier in the day. The best part of all of this is that they are cognitively aware of all of it. We've taken the explosiveness out of it and it is working.

Cooperation over competition is not an easy task! It's as if my students have been raised on competition. They don't know how to trust each other enough to work cooperatively. I don't think they've had enough exposure to working together and I realized that groups need guidelines and practice. We are still working on moving past the group dynamics where one student does all the work and the others chat. By letting group members know that they will all be asked questions about their work and be expected to answer, I've closed the gap somewhat. However, I still find that they just don't know how to talk through problems together. I wish I had done more on showing them what "good" groups look like.

A classroom where achievement is valued is like a well-oiled machine! And it is one filled with hope. I think the full inclusion fits in here, too. All students achieving creates kind of a current and it pulls everyone along. They may float along at a different place and end up at a different point in the river, but they all have downstream movement! What an analogy—kind of cheesy. Sorry!

The note about rules and not posting consequences next to standards or expectations of behavior is completely on point. Kids will always find the flaw. It is their favorite thing to do! And I love that about them. I do the same exact thing! It's like the dress code. They are all trying to find the loophole.

We all find that transitions are the most difficult times in a classroom. This feels like free time to students unless there is a procedure or protocol for how to do it. Our cohort does this during our Saturday classes! I find so much that my students need affection, but sternness. They need rules, but freedom. They need an agenda, but no stress. It's such a thin line to walk.

The Community slide is exactly what I believe. I do my best to check my own negative emotions or to at least be honest with students if I am "having a bad day." I have often had students tell me that they could tell something was wrong, but they didn't know I was in a bad mood, which I find odd in a way. I have had the opportunity to get to know my students in an authentic way. I know some secrets and I've been privileged to spend a lot of time just talking about their experiences with them. They really like to talk about themselves and to hear about my experiences. Once a class was really out of control and I started talking (basically to myself) about how it breaks my heart to watch healthy, smart kids not take their education seriously. I droned on about how parents in India pay an entire year's worth of salary that they earn scrubbing other people's toilets to send their kids to a school where the teacher actually shows up. The room quieted down so I continued to talk about watching 4-year-old kids carry rocks during road construction and 10-year-old girls who were in charge of making dinner...on a metal plate and an open fire. It drew them in and we were able to connect. They see that I am here because I want them to succeed and to get everything they are entitled to as an American citizen. I've also really encouraged them to think about the Peace Corps or any volunteer organization that would give them the chance to see other cultures and to walk in someone else's shoes.

My put down plan is "minus five." My students now "snitch" on each other when they use one of the "Don't Go There Words." I made it clear that I didn't like the F-word and that it was not to be used in my room. I also put the N-word and "gay" on the list. I know my students' voices and I don't even break stride. I just call out "minus five" and move on. I keep track on a clipboard. Students can earn 20 points for being polite, i.e. not using those words, or they can lose them. But as I tell them, you have the 20 points when you walk in the door. I give them the benefit of the doubt. It's up to them to keep them or lose them.

My kids are so quick to escalate a conflict. I try role playing a lot to make them see the other perspective. I have been the principal, the bad kid, the mom, the mean teacher, the friend, and the students involved in conflict. There is always a humorous part because I think that laughter helps dissipate the anger or hurt. Humor gives me an "in" to talk to the student and not at him or her. I strive to have resolution before students leave my classroom or, if it happened outside my class, to give them some tools for working through it. I think it would be great to have counselors come in and talk about anger management and conflict negotiation.

Teacher Reflection Five

Brain Reflection

One of the main points that struck me in this PowerPoint is the slide that focuses on meeting a child's basic needs. I often understand how it is hard for my students to focus on math when their basic physiological needs are not being met according to Maslow's Hierarchy. I often have students who put their heads down because they were up late the night before taking care of their little brother or had a headache that was due to a lack of food and nutrients. It's hard to see my students have so much going on in their personal lives that school is often an escape or refuge from the world outside. They all announce when they have food stamps, because it means they are finally getting a "full fridge." It's hard to separate myself as their teacher. I bring food as rewards for good behavior and my students are often so grateful for the treats and incredibly motivated by food. I am often saddened by how little my students have and how often they ask me if I have anything to eat since they "didn't eat breakfast" or only "eat at school."

As a way to not let myself fall victim to making excuses for my students and to ensure I maintain high expectations, I have a routine that students are able to follow and expect. It's amazing how often students will grab their own interactive notebooks and pass them out if I was busy talking to another student after class and will ask where the "Do Now" is if I haven't put it up before the bell rings to start class. I really do feel that a teacher's beliefs are manifested in their teaching and classroom environment. My students know that I believe they can achieve success in math, but that it will require work. I expect them to do the work I ask and always offer help and support when needed. I always squash any negative comments about "never getting math" or being "dumb" because I tell my students that they can do math and are smart. I also try to cater to the different learners in my classroom and give students points for completion and not just accuracy to further reward those who put in the effort necessary to excel in school.

I do agree with the quote from Harry Wong, that a lack of procedures is the main issue in the classroom. I've learned this school year that set procedures help students know how to behave and set expectations for their behaviors. I've also learned how important consistency and following through is. When I make a promise, or threat, I need to consistently enforce it; otherwise my students will not behave in the manner I desire. I feel the classroom community also helps with behavior as students can either promote or eliminate another student's outburst or cry for attention. I often have students tell others to stop talking because they want to listen and learn.

As much as I try to make my learning environment safe, I find it extremely difficult to implement group work into my daily lessons, even with set procedures. My poor attendance, lack of motivation, and extreme diversity in skill level (which often results in low self-esteem and a student will shut down in group settings) make it hard for students to experience the benefits of cooperative learning. My students constantly inform me that they prefer individual work, and don't seem to enjoy games. I know it is partially related to their lack of belief in their own talents and skills. As a Title Math Class, my students often insult themselves and lack of success and make it a reason for not trying. They are embarrassed when they do not understand a topic and are often embarrassed to be in my class because of the negative connotation associated with it. As a result, I do agree with the presentation that emphasizes promoting community. Although group work hasn't been successful in my classroom, my students know that I expect kind words and want them to leave their social judgments and commitments outside of my classroom.

Teacher Reflection Six

Brain Compatible Learning and Learner-Centered Education

As a first-year teacher, I have found out a lot about myself and have grown as a person at a steady rate. I believe my strong understanding of psychology is my strongest asset as a teacher and this Power Point on brain compatible learning and learner-centered education has only provided strong evidence about this belief.

Students must feel safe and secure to maximize their abilities to engage and novelty and joyfulness contribute to engagement according to the Power Point. I strongly agree with this research because I have developed a reputation at my school that I have really strong relationships with my students and I believe these strong relationships are a result of the beliefs I developed when I decided to become a teacher. I believed that the most important part of my job as a teacher was to develop good relationships with my students. Using my strong interest and understanding of psychology, I knew that the basis of developing strong relationships with others is through consistency, patience, and effort.

From the first day I met my students through the day I wrote this paper, I have made a conscious effort to be consistent in my actions around students and have allowed them to feel comfortable to be themselves around me without judging them. This consistent behavior I have displayed has created a true friendship between my students and I, which has resulted in engaged learning and high performances on scrimmages, benchmarks, and many other assessments.

Teacher Reflection Seven

Do my assumptions drive my classroom systems?

Although there were many interesting parts to this Power Point, this small section on assumptions really stood out for me. I definitely trust my students much more than my colleagues and overall it hasn't backfired yet. Sure my days are hectic with "study-hall-stragglers" every class period, a million notes/stories/favors every passing period, classes full of anxious students needing my attention, and icy attitudes from colleagues who are put off by my popularity. But, students genuinely like my class and my style and I've had many successes with "troubled" students that only work in my class and for me. My classroom is loose and fun. I am proud that my classes love to identify it as "3rd period!" One class even made t-shirts touting their pride to surprise me. I also love that my kids are friends with classmates in my class but have little to nothing to do with each other outside of class. Getting along with the kids has been a breeze, it's my colleagues that have been the challenge. Sure we're cordial to each other, but there is a wall between us and until this Power Point I wasn't sure why. I have fundamental disagreements with them about our assumptions we make of our students. I trust the students and treat them like actual people. Some other teachers treat them like numbers. Don't get me wrong, our school has many wonderful teachers, but there feels to be some very competitive and icy teachers who are harder to deal with than many students.

My technique is not without its own flaws. I think I might over-value my relationships with students and their relationships with each other, more than I value my content. Many days I feel like a great team leader, guidance counselor, coach, team mate, preacher; and occasionally a good science teacher. My goal is to blend the two. I've had some really great days where my energy was funneled into very successful lessons. I just haven't figured out a way to be consistent with this. I guess I need to spend even more time lesson planning. When I love a lesson, I can sell it to them easily. When a lesson is so-so or even weak, then I don't feel like doing it and I just kind of plow through.

Teacher Reflection Eight

When I was going over the Power Point from January on the brain, a couple points truly hit home. First of all, the point that our classrooms and schools must be a safe haven for our students really hit home for me. A couple of times this year I felt that I had an opportunity to provide that safe haven for a couple of my students, but failed to do so. I have regretted these missed opportunities since, even though I have protected other students in other situations. I think that one missed opportunity to protect students can be catastrophic to the relationship building process with that student as well as make the process with the other students in the classroom much more difficult. For this reason and because I believe that, ultimately, it is my responsibility to make certain my classroom is safe for all of my students, I will carry my failures here with me for my entire career.

The second point that I would like to discuss is that of ODD. I believe that I truly see this exhibited in my classroom more than it is diagnosed. I don't believe that I handle situations where this is manifested well in most instances. It is definitely easier to become confrontational than to do the right thing here and stay calm. After reading the notes, I will certainly make a stronger effort to approach situations with these students in a more appropriate and delicate way.

Last Reflection: Lori's Reflection

December 2011

Completing this book has brought to mind three distinct notions I desire to include in this reflection. First, I am by no means an expert in educational reform and instructional mastery, but this manuscript has gratefully reminded me I remain a constant student of learning and life. There is much to question, wonder, and celebrate inside this ever-expanding system of an educational conundrum within a world of extreme diversity and contrast. It will be the plasticity of my perspective that leads the way to a natural balance of mind and heart intelligence where "how-to" books on any subject cannot reach!

Secondly, I envision the day when our children and adolescents will be upheld for all the imaginative genius and compassion they hold coming into this world. Our children are ingenious creators who feel empowered before they enter into this mystery of education. If we allowed them to express who they are with less constraints and human-created rules and regulations, I believe they would not go astray. They would maintain worthiness and innate feelings of well-being with gentle guidance and affirmations of all that is going well.

Finally, as I write and teach, I have embraced the power and magnificence of *perspective* as a lens of change. When life experiences are presented with accompanying feelings of joy, sadness, frustration, angst, and fear, we embrace the tool and strategy that is our inherent birthright, *perspective*. It engineers and creates paths of freedom, happiness and peaceful resolution when we take the time to implement its muscle. Perspective drives every moment of each day and is capable of creating the positive changes we desire in our lives when we put it into practice and allow.

~ Lori L. Desautels

Compassionate Presence, National Standard

Compassion and Collaboration—How will these standards be incorporated in our classrooms and across curriculum?

Key Ideas and Details

1. Students will begin to understand how compassion creates an awareness of the world around them, acknowledging different cultures and perspectives. In this highly connected and digital age, the learned skill of *compassionate presence* is an essential skill, because being able to understand what others are experiencing and acting on their behalf raises the level of emotional, cognitive and social learning.

2. With the initiation into the understanding of the power of positive thought and service to another, students and educators will begin to engage the mind and heart with clarity, understanding, and acceptance through class discussions, specific reading materials, such as folklores and mythology, and service assignments within the community.

3. The study and implementation of Self-Explanatory Styles through the research and study of Dr. Martin Seligman's work in Positive Psychology will assist students and teachers in deeply understanding how their thoughts and words drive their behaviors inside everyday experiences.

Comprehension and Collaboration—How will these standards be incorporated in our classrooms and across curriculum?

1. Engage in a range of collaborative discussions (one-on-one), small groups, and teacher- and student-led demonstrations, sharing personal examples of acts of compassion contrasted with

examples and experiences of what is and feels violent, hateful and selfish to oneself and to others.

2. Texts for reading and discussion groups formed to assist in discussing one's values, ideas, and feelings. These discussion groups will be embedded into core subjects:

Primary—ages 5-10—*The Giving Tree, Unexpected Treasure, Milton's Secret* and *The Quiltmaker's Gift.*

Middle School and Secondary Texts—*Understanding How Other People Operate, Middle School and High School Field of Compassion, Karen Armstrong and the 12 Steps of Compassion.*

Presentation of Knowledge and Ideas/Curriculum Outline in Each Grade Level

1. Educators and students begin modeling service to one another and therefore oneself, through asking the questions through-out the day: *How may I serve you? What do you need? How can I help?*

2. "Deep Listening" begins when we engage with another, feeling his or her emotions. This is a critical skill and component when students and educators find themselves in disagreements or stuck in perpetual negative situations. Deep listening is the skill and act that enables us to step out of our own thoughts and feelings, experiencing the feelings, perspectives, and thoughts of another. We place our feelings and thoughts aside when we listen beneath the words and behaviors of one another.

3. Whole class, small groups or individuals create an array of options, perspectives, and incremental steps and goals that lead to resolution when conflict is present. We will integrate strategies in assisting students, parents and educators to separate the actions and behaviors from the person who is struggling with choices.

Brainstorming lists, mind-mapping and group collaboration are a few of the strategies that will assist in this compassionate process.

4. Understand how the power of thoughts, perspectives, and feelings drives our attention, mental clarity and ability to learn and master the academic standards and benchmarks. "Perspective study" begins in kindergarten and continues through the student's senior year in high school as research and experience demonstrates perspective drives how we perceive life and every situation we create and experience.

5. Exercises of gratitude begin each day in every classroom. Students and educators will spend three to four minutes discussing, writing, and exploring the many ways to appreciate every aspect of their lives. When integrating the art and science of gratitude, students will begin each day cultivating positive emotion when appreciating one or two aspects in their present lives while envisioning what is possible.

6. Strength Training—Educators and students will discuss and explore individual strengths and aptitudes of students through-out each semester, incorporating an active list while graphing these strengths and aptitudes into Individual Learning Plans to be reviewed, shared, and implemented throughout the school year.

7. The compassionate presence standard proficiency will be demonstrated through a performance-based assessment collaboratively selected by schools, classrooms, students and parents. These performance-based assessments will vary based on student interests, cultures, aptitudes, prior knowledge and personal understanding.

Elementary National Compassionate Standard

1. Introduction to our commonalities as people and a discussion of gratitude each morning in community gatherings. Students

will spend three or four minutes appreciating and forming positive aspects of one another and themselves.

2. How may I serve you? What do you need? How can I help? What could be different? How are you feeling? Students and educators will be asked to create two projects during the school year (collectively) that will serve a family, organization, or individual. The students, parents and teachers will integrate these projects into national standards so that reading, math, social sciences and science and are enriched and learned deeply for formative and summative assessment purposes.

3. Critical thinking skills and perspective exercises will be introduced as the driving forces for understanding thought formation while discovering positive emotion even inside a difficult or challenging situation.

4. Discussions will be required about real life famous heroes—stories of well known, compassionate individuals who have contributed to the well-being of societies in modeling moral values, hearty leadership and authenticity of thought and effort. Compassionate leaders like the Dalai Lama, Mahatma Gandhi, and Martin Luther King, Jr. who are renowned for their compassion and moral attitudes will be a few of the many individuals discussed and shared.

5. Mind-sight strategies created by Dr. Dan Siegel promoting focused attention will be integrated into every classroom through all schools. These strategies will be taught to both educators and students, with outcomes assessed for lessening chronic stress, increasing clarity of thought, and promoting empathy for one another so collaborative teaching and learning becomes a model of best practice.

6. Conflict Resolution will become a way of relational learning. All students and teachers will model how to detach the "prob-

lem" from the individual as options, possibilities, solutions and brainstorming with an array of perspectives will create responsible and accountable students and teachers.

Secondary National Compassionate Standard

1. Relational Learning will continue through a focus on cooperation rather than competition. Students and educators will be asked to take perspectives of various cultures, beliefs, and family heritages worldwide to deepen understanding and knowledge of those human differences—perspectives will be explored as this relates to content, standards and future professional roles. This knowledge will be generated through the following:

A. International pen pals and correspondence—sharing ideas, feelings and thoughts revolving around education and living life.

B. Incarcerated individuals—what choices did they make to get where they are? What could change? How could their situations change? What thoughts contributed to their placement in this time? How will it improve?

C. Through student, parent and educator forums, thoughts, feelings and perspectives will be explored relating to brain health, individual happiness and mindful learning, in which focused attention becomes a natural characteristic and component of all learning and teaching.

2. Gratitude will be taught and expressed throughout school days, with this concept being interspersed within the academic curriculum. Journals will be kept for all students to draw, write and personally express gratitude and appreciation for even the most difficult and tenuous school and home experiences.

3. Service Projects—Grade levels within each school will be held accountable for service to individuals, organizations or groups of persons within the community who are in need of assis-

tance. Each grade level will complete two service projects throughout the school year showcasing their projects and reflections with local government, school boards, parents, educators and other students within the district.

4. Senior Service—Public school second semester seniors will work in the community for a service organization 20 hours per week with a performance-based project designed to reflect and highlight service experiences for graduation credit. These projects will be approved by faculty, school boards, and the state departments of educational instruction for dual credit applied to higher education or shared with future employees during the interview process affecting successful job placement. A committee of students, parents, educators, and outside businesses will assess and give feedback for each project.

The Voices of Our Students' Hearts

Student Poetry

Disappointment #2

Home is dark and cold
My brother betrayed me
The pain, the sorrow, the disappointment of my dad
Eyes blood shot red from crying
 Hatred for my brother

Alone, lied to, secretive, torn apart
9 years old and you are gone
Dad why are you leaving, I'm just going to the bar with John
"Imma be back", dad don't leave
Upstairs crying in my bed

Wondering if you're going to come back
Dad you're my best friend, can't live without you
My brother hurt me and I can't tell you
I'm disappointed I've been betrayed
Sorry that's all you say but I don't take it
You say it all the time but I need more
You're my brother but I don't claim you
Because you are a disappointment you're nothing to me
Aaron you're shady

~Tyisha

As If in a Dream

I've never found something so bizarre
Watching myself fall in so far
Observing clips of my haunting past
When I was treating everything like it was some useless trash

I've moved on so why must I see this yet again
Falling in so far, falling in so deep
Am I dreaming, could I be asleep?
I must be, but everything feels and seems so real
Seeing flying arks, dragons, and other mythical creatures

My eyes can no longer keep the deal of seeing what's true
Everything is beginning to turn as dark as night
I shall soon be as blind as a bat
I must believe, I must wake and drop off the haunting truths
and imaginary lies
I must go the distance

Finally to come in contact to the floor
Holding my glory within my hands
I make a stand to only face what stands underneath me

Looking through its eyes with its twisted face
I begin to wonder could this be my fate
The floor then begins to act as an earthquake
Then a lightning bolt comes down with a roaring flash

Last thing I remember I was floating at the surface of a lake
To find out that I was finally awake

~Anthony

Dreaming Big Is Harmless

I imagine a place of complete silence…
Police cars cease to exist because people don't murder
Enemies are a forgotten past because gun shots murmur
Racism is no more because we are in this together
And those depressing, rainy days become bright, sunny weather

I imagine a world of religious guidance…
Poor is no longer a state of mind because we believe
Addicts don't grieve because the narcotics leave
Sins are washed away and rarely return
Because family becomes our only major concern

I imagine a place of no worries…
Next month's rent is never dreaded.
And years of debt can finally be shredded
Everyone is employed because jobs are abundant,
Leading to exploration ending days that are redundant.

High above reality dreaming up another earth,
Wishing I could be there; a mind rebirth.
Even though reality stops my fantasy's existence.
As long as I dream big,
It will gain persistence.
Dreaming…is believing.

~ Jeremiah

Quiet Storm

Our love is the ocean…
So quiet, tranquil, calm
But yet so unpredictable
As we drift along without purpose,
So many problems waiting just over the horizon,

Sometimes the moon causes our relationship to climax,
Causing a sudden rage of destruction,
Devastation so unimaginable,
But no regrets.
No explanation to why.
We watch memories pass over
Like a terrible storm
Myriads of watery graves..
In the bottomless abyss

We're uncontrollable, unbalanced
Drowning in the arguments,
Falling deeper into the dark, struggle
Deeper into depression
Where we lose sight and hearing,
like plunging into a pool of water
 of sad, sudden silence

Our eyes fall back,
as we take one last look
at the peaceful harmony we shared
Slowly drifting apart as we perish,
Falling deeper, deeper
And deeper.

~ Jeremiah

Feeling for you

I know don't think you love
I don't feel the love for me is within you
I hate that you talk about me
Saying things about me that aren't true
Soon you will pay for your mistakes
When I am gone and out of your life
When I leave don't be sad
Because you caused this to happen
My heart loves but my mind hates
Which should I believe
Should I think about loving
Or should I just love
When you wrap your arms around me
I feel warm and protected
Having the feeling of protection when you hold me tightly
The sounds of your voice
You telling me you love me
So should we be together
If your love is in my heart

~ Jahkeem

Forever Mine

There was a girl u met
That I know would forever be
Mine I met her when I was 7
Every time she spoke
She blew my mind just
To hear her rhymes would make
Me smile.
When we grew older I
Saw her change into a
New woman the girl I
Fell in love with was no
Longer there all of her purity
Was gone. Everybody
Thought they could use her but her body
Was only for the best
Now when I see or hear her
Speak its hard for me
To feel the same way I
Felt when I was 7
Dang how times have changed
Even when I her speak
She just doesn't sound the
Same I miss her the young real
Cut throat girl
I miss the real her like Bobby miss Whitney
Tell me if you seen her hip-hop

~ Marcus

Roller Coaster

Love is like a roller coaster ride.
You stand around waiting in line,
The whole time wondering is this even worth the wait.
But you're really working up the nerve to get on.
So you've decided to ride.
You get butterflies once you get in, and haven't even moved
yet.
Before you know it, it starts to move,
That's when you realize it's too late to get off,
But do you want to.
You're having fun its exciting
You're moving fast, yeah it's a bit bumpy but you don't mind.
You see the first hill ahead,
You think to yourself how beautiful it looks from the view,
You feel as though you're on top of the world,
never noticing the drop ahead.
Until you fall.
You feel it in the pit of your stomach, it makes you sick.
You curse, you pray, you cry, you scream to get off.
You pull up to the platform, and BAM! It's over. Just like that!
As you exit the very thing that made you wait around, laugh,
took you high and dropped you,
All you're thinking is, "I wanna do it again!"

~ Kenya

Love Shouldn't Hit

Love shouldn't hit
Why do you hit me
Why do you beat me every day and every night?
You say u love me
You clam you mii baby
You say you want to marry me
When I don't do what you say
You get very mad
If were in public
You won't do anything
But when were at home or behind close doors
You treat me like a whore
You force me to do things to you that I don't at all
If I refuse to do them
You abuse me
So there's one more thing I have to say
Do you really love me
Or do u love the fact that you can abuse me
Day n nite

~ Jasmine

Music

Music at times is a hard thing to deal with
All of the instruments, notes, beats and lyrics
It's always easy when you begin the process
All fun and a smile that looked like it ran for miles and miles.
But once you get over that period of lust everything seems
entirely different from what it was
The notes that once sounded so beautifully
Now have you trying to figure out what else there is to play

Seems like the music is becoming more irrelevant
Trying to remember when you last felt this beat in your heart
Why this music appealed to you from the start
The music that once made you light up
Is now the music that makes you want to give up?
Give up on music
Give up on instruments
Maybe even give up on rhythm

The lyrics that were once so sweet and loving
Are now speaking awful and bitter words that leave you
wanting nothing
Wanting nothing more to do with music
Or nothing but to be left alone
The chorus has been changed
Those sweet lyrics are no longer the same
The notes you once had
Have become a faded memory of the past
The rhythm you once danced to
Is now like gum on the bottom of your shoe
The kind that's been there for a while and melts

on a hot summer's day
So even when you try it's hard to walk away.
Sad to say things never stay the same,
The lyrics once spoken can easily be changed.
So when you begin new music,
After the last beat decided to walk out of your life.
Remember music is going to be a hard thing to deal with,
Especially instruments, notes, beats and lyrics.

~ Stania

Progress

Let's go back and be
Anti-progressive.
Burn Computers
Unmoved civil rights,
Undestroy Dresden.
Deliberate women
Forget voting

Have Edison lose the light.
Declare our dependence, make
All men created unequal.
Give us the rights to
Death, slavery, and the pursuit of misery.

Unrape the Native Americans
And their land.
While we're at it...

Unland on Pride Rock,
Undrop Pride Rock from on Africa,
Unsplit the church,
Unseek the Holy Grail,
Uncrusade the Holy Land,
Uncricify the Holy One,
Unconquor the Middle East.

Do it again,
And again.
And again.

Are we to the Babylonians yet?

Dry out the great flood,
And un-eat knowledge.
Almost there…
Un-bang the universe.

Until all we're left with is
The sucking sound a straw makes
When the lemonade we've made
From these Lemons is gone.
And we're left,
Waiting for the waiter
To give us something less tart.

~ Joel Thomas
Educator , Indianapolis, Indiana

The Truth About Coffee Houses

I see you with your
Delpha
Mac book
Iphone
Briefcase
And I saw you pull up in your eco-friendly car
Why do I care?
Because you say you are going green
But you were just smoking out back hell I still smell it over
your overpriced fragrance
You say you love kids
But missed all of your only nephews birthdays
You say you are vegan
But your latte has milk in it
You say you are here to work on your book in peace
But you are really here to do your promoting for
your new book
But I see you with your drink, macbook, iphone, briefcase, and
eco-friendly car!

~ Ashley

This is War

Enraged like a dragon with no heart,
I am the color red;
your eyes are the color of fear,
in a never-ending battle between good and evil,
who will win?
Make sure you take everything you hold dear,
Your loved ones aren't going where you're going,
Here I am,
I am as close to you as your skin,
Hope is only a simile,
Not real only something to compare to your mere strength,
I bleed rain,
I laugh when you are in pain,
My name is the face you see in the mirror every day,
Behind you I tell you what you can and cannot do,
I watch you closely,
Making sure if you make a mistake,
I constantly tell you all day
I wonder if I'm insane,
I'm sorry I can't help the way God made me,
Being born with bull's horns is a benefit,
A disadvantage for you,
I will watch you when you fall,
Horns will be the last thing you see,
Exhaustion is only a dream,
Silently I'll watch you like a shark in deep water,
Pray for your final minute,
Or only just a few spare moments of extra breath,
Tears will do you no good,
The armies have played there final horn,
Be gone now friend,
Death is imminent to come,
Now my battle is won

~ Bolanle

Three Stages of Pain

My pain is something I can't express
It's something I try and hold in
I try release this stress off my chest
But it's like an uncontrollable wind

My emotional pain is like someone has hidden it from me
I feel like I'm surfing a wave, that I can't rely on
It's somewhere underwater captured by the sea
It's something that you will never in a million years
feast your eyes on

My mental pain explains how I'm a mystery
It keeps all my memories stored in my mind
It shows my background and history
It shows how I'm at the top and not behind

When I feel my physical pain it is a feeling
that's hit me and makes me feel numb
I can't help but to hold it in and let it heal
When I hold it in I feel so stupid and dumb
I want to let it out because the pain that I feel
is like eating an upsetting meal

~Jaylin

End Notes

1. Gatto, John Taylor. *Dumbing Us Down*. Gabriola Island, BC, Canada: New Society Publishers, 2008. p.19.

2. Pink, Daniel. *A Whole New Mind*. New York: Penguin Group, 2006. p.1.

3. Ibid., p.1.

4. Wolfe, Pat. *Mind Matters, Inc.* Retrieved from <http://patwolfe.com>

5. Cutler, Howard, MD, and His Holiness, The Dalai Lama. *The Art of Happiness in a Troubled World*. Doubleday, 2009. P. XV1

6. Ibid., p.169

7. Chopra, Deepak. *The Ultimate Happiness Prescription*. Harmony Books, 2009. p. 131.

8. Ibid., p. 61.

9. Ibid., p.136.

10. Ibid., p.137.

11. Cutler, Howard, MD, and His Holiness, The Dalai Lama. *The Art of Happiness in a Troubled World*. Doubleday, 2009. p. 3.

12. Robinson, Sir Ken. *The Element*. Viking Adult, 2009. p. 230, p.83.

13. Ibid., p.21.

14. Pink, Daniel. *A Whole New Mind*. New York: Penguin Group, 2006. p. 2-3.

15. Ibid., p. 2-3.

16. Ibid., p.17.

17. Robinson, Sir Ken. *The Element*. Viking Adult, 2009. p. 254.

18. Valle, Jan W., and Conner, David J. *Rethinking Disability*. McGraw Hill Publishing, 2010. p.65.

19. Robinson, Sir Ken. *The Element*. Viking Adult, 2009. p. 255.

20. Jensen, Eric. *Different brains, Different Learners* (second edition). Corwin press, 2010., p. 56.

21. 21 Ibid., p.56.

22. Foster, Peter. (2010, Feb., 3). *Third of Chinese Primary School Children Suffer Stress, Study Finds*. Retrieved from <http://telegraph.co.uk>

23. Childre, Doc, and Rozman, Deborah. *Transforming Anger*. New Harbinger Publications, 2003, p. 5.

24. Ibid., p.5.

25. Goode, Caron. *More 4 Kids*. Teaching Compassion to Children, Retrieved from <http://more4kids.info>

26. Seigel, Dan, MD. *Mindsight*. Bantam Books, 2010. p.62-63.

27. Kozol, Jonathan. *Letters to a Young Teacher.* Crown Publishers, 2007. p.19.

28. TeachingAmericanHistory.org, a project of the Ashbrook Center at Ashland University. <http://teachingamericanhistory.org>

29. Palmer, Parker. *The Courage to Teach.* Jossey-Bass Publishing, 1997. p.11.

30. Kotter, John. (April 12, 2006). *The Power of Stories,* Retrieved from <http://www.Forbes.com>

31. Kozol, Jonathan. *On Being A Teacher.* One World Publication, 1993, reprinted 2009. p.20.

32. Pink, Daniel. *A Whole New Mind.* New York: Penguin Group, 2006, p.49.

33. Cameron, Brent. *Self-Design.* Sentient Publications, 2006, p.19.

34. Arbinger Institute. *The Anatomy of Peace.* Berrett-Koehker Publishers, 2008, p.37.

35. Kaufeldt, Martha. *Begin With The Brain.* Corwin Press, 2010, p.2.

36. Cutler, Howard, MD, and His Holiness, The Dalai Lama. *The Art of Happiness in a Troubled World.* Doubleday, 2009, p.259.

37. Ibid., pp. 267-269.

38. Seligman, Martin. *Authentic Happiness, Department of Positive Psychology, University of Pennsylvania.* Retrieved from <http://www.ppc.sas.upenn.edu/ppintroarticle.pdf>

39. Seligman, Martin, E.P. *Learned Optimism*. Vintage Books, 2006, p.16.

40. Emmons, Robert A., and McCullough, Michael E. Counting blessings versus burdens: An experimental investigation of gratitude and subjective well-being in daily life. *Journal of Personality and Social Psychology* Vol 84(2), Feb 2003, 377-389.

41. Faber, Adele, and Mazlish, Elaine. *How to Talk So Kids Will Listen and Listen So Kids Will Talk*. Rawson, Wade Publishers, 1980, p.18.

42. Wallis, Claudia. (2005, Jan., 17). The New Science of Happiness. *Time Magazine* Retrieved from <http://www.authentichappiness.sas.upenn.edu>

43. Palmer, Parker. *The Courage to Teach*. Jossey-Bass, 1998, p.1.

44. Cutler, Howard, MD, and His Holiness, The Dalai Lama. *The Art of Happiness in a Troubled World*. Doubleday, 2009, p. 327.

Made in the USA
Lexington, KY
22 May 2019